MY DOG'S NAME
IS EINSTEIN

Michael Kalafatas and Susan Simon

MY DOG'S NAME IS EINSTEIN

AND OTHER COLLEGE ESSAYS
WRITTEN FROM THE HEARTS
OF BOYS AND GIRLS

Admissions Advantage

WESTON, MA

FIRST VINTAGE EDITION
JUNE 2010

To each new generation of young people who aspire to college and begin a journey of self-discovery.

ABOUT THE AUTHORS

Michael Kalafatas

Michael Kalafatas served for thirty-five years as a college admissions officer, two thirds of that time as Director of Admissions at Brandeis University. Since 2002 he has counseled students and their families on all aspects of the college admissions process as an educational adviser at Admissions Advantage in Weston, MA. He is the author of two books: THE BELLSTONE: *The Greek Sponge Divers of the Aegean, One American's Journey Home* (2003, Brandeis University Press and the University Press of New England) and BIRD STRIKE: *The Crash of the Boston Electra* (2010, same publishers). He has written magazine articles on varied topics, including college admissions. He was also executive producer of the film, "Pushing the Limits," based on THE BELLSTONE, now part of the marine science film series, Immersion Presents, created by underwater explorer Dr. Robert Ballard. Across his professional life Michael has been in high demand as a public speaker in the US and abroad on college admissions topics and topics related to his writing. He has made numerous appearances on radio and television in the US and overseas. He holds a B.A. in politics from Brandeis and a Master in Arts in Teaching degree from Harvard.

Susan Simon

Susan Simon is the founder of Admissions Advantage - created to support students and families as they make their way through the college admissions process. The counseling firm's mission is to prepare students for admission to college through self-discovery and character development rather than just by the accumulating of a long list of activities. With eighteen years of experience as an educator and admissions officer, Susan Simon provides students and families with wise counsel and practical expertise. Previously, Susan worked for eighteen years as Senior Admissions Counselor at Brandeis University interviewing thousands of students and reading over 100,000 applications and making admissions decisions. Susan holds a B.S. in Education degree from Wheelock College, well known for their work in child development, and an M.A. in Counseling Psychology from Santa Clara University. She has been a certified guidance counselor and an elementary school teacher. She currently serves on the Executive Committee and is Vice Chair of the Wheelock College Board of Trustees. She also holds an honorary doctoral degree from Wheelock. Her professional affiliations include memberships in the National Association for College Admissions Counseling and the Independent Educational Consultants Association.

ACKNOWLEDGMENTS

We would like to thank Lisa Giles, Joe McCoy and Suzy Stayman of Admissions Advantage who act as champions in helping students find stories that only they can tell. Many thanks as well to Cyana Chilton, Joyce Gordon and Jerri Shaer who helped in the preparation of this book.

TABLE OF CONTENTS

INTRODUCTION

ESSAYS FROM THE HEARTS OF BOYS

Essays from the Hearts of Girls

MY DOG'S NAME IS EINSTEIN AND OTHER COLLEGE ESSAYS

INTRODUCTION

Childhood experiences and your memories of them are at the core of who you are today. Taking time to daydream and indulge in memories - starting from the very beginning - is integral to writing a college essay.

LETTING THE FUTURE IN

Do you remember how cozy you felt when you snuggled next to your dad in your favorite pair of pajamas or when you laced up your first pair of brand-new soccer cleats and marched onto the field? What was it like when you found a best friend or went off to camp for the first time? Do you remember the day you came home after sledding down hills at breakneck speed and were greeted by your dog and your mom with a cup of hot cocoa? How incredibly challenging was it when you wrote your first 15-page research paper on the Civil War or worked a summer job as a cashier at the grocery store down the street? Childhood experiences and your memories of them are at the core of who you are today. These questions hold important and meaningful answers. In MY DOG'S NAME IS EINSTEIN, we are asking you to explore the answers to questions like these. Taking time to daydream and indulge in memories - starting from the very beginning - will help you in applying to college. We promise that the journey back in time will be fun and lead to results even beyond your childhood dreams. Sit back, relax, and enjoy the stories we offer from kids just like you. We hope that you find inspiration in the essays and that they guide you in finding your own amazing stories and help you look into your future. But first some advice from former college admissions officers and also some advice that you might even recall from childhood stories that were read to you long ago...

FINDING YOUR OWN KEY

Lewis Carroll, author of Alice in Wonderland, had a special fondness for keys and padlocks, and they often appeared in his fantasies. In one of these a padlock with long spidery legs races to and fro in quite a dither, exclaiming, "I'm looking for the key that unlocks me!" Such is the cry of youth. Such is the cry of us all at times.

In MY DOG'S NAME IS EINSTEIN we present a collection of magical, mystical, and magnificent college essays written by young people who looked for - and found - "the key that unlocks me." And that discovery made all the difference - in their college search, college essays, college interviews, and, most important, in their confidence that the compass headings selected, as they began their college admissions journeys, were the correct ones. Like little Milo in The Phantom Tollbooth, driving his magical car, these students had entered "The Land of Expectations," which can be a frightening and confusing place, but they now understood that when you travel to a new and important destination, it helps if you know where you are going. The young authors in this book had learned, before beginning their journeys, to pause and search "for the key that unlocks me"; they had learned the prudence of taking an inward journey before taking any great outward journey. They had learned the wisdom of that old Spanish proverb, "A man blind to his own nation will never know where he is traveling."

The novelist Graham Greene, who knew a great deal about new adventure, once wrote, "There is a moment in childhood when a door opens and lets the future in." Applying to college can be that moment, if realized and the golden moment gathered in. As college admissions decision-makers across decades and now college advisers joyously at work with young people and families in the throes of college admissions, we hope through this book to help students and their families "let the future in." In three ways.

First, by assembling for your scrutiny college essays that do what a college essay is supposed to do: Answer a college admissions officer's top question in reading an application essay. What's he like? What's she like? And also answer the next most important question an admissions officer asks: Can the student write?

Second, we want to share with you a view from our long-occupied perch, not discussed elsewhere: young men and young women often approach the college essay differently. Not always but often. Their core values are not dramatically different from one another, for we don't have to think alike to aspire alike or to tremble alike as we leave home for this first time. But we will let you be the judge of what role gender might play, or might not play, as you read these wonderful essays in MY DOG'S NAME IS EINSTEIN.

Third, and most important, we want to show you how one looks for "the key that unlocks me." Not with the mind, but with the heart. "One sees clearly only with the heart," says the fox in St. Exupery's The Little Prince, a book for children of all ages and a wise life guide. "Anything essential is invisible to the eyes," adds the fox. But we have practical advice for you too. We want to help you find the key that nicely fits: your own key. As another of Lewis Carroll's characters, The Professor, sagely notes, "I have observed that a door opens much more nicely with its own key."

Admissions officers love numbers, it's true - grade point averages, national testing results, and all the like - except when it comes to the college essay (and college interview). That is where they set numbers aside and hope a student will open a window and let them see the world the way the student sees it. The college essay is the place where what a student cares about can be revealed, where a student's personality and character can shine through, where childhood dreams can be put up on the big screen for all to see. As Professor Randy Pausch said, in his now famous lecture, *Really Achieving Your Childhood Dreams*, "the inspiration and permission to dream is huge," as he urged us all to pursue our childhood dreams. And, he adds, "remember brick walls are there for a reason. . . to give us a chance to show how badly we want something. Because the brick walls are there to stop the people who don't want it badly enough. They're there to stop the other people." College admissions officers want to know about your hopes and your childhood dreams, what you value, and, especially, the person you are becoming. Realize they don't want a finished product; otherwise, you'd have nothing to do when you got to their college. They want to know the person you are becoming.

Admissions officers often act like the grown-ups in The Little Prince; a little disappointing and dreary, with all their counting and measuring. But not when it comes to the college essay when they're quite nicely like the children in The Little Prince; they too want to know what's really important about a new person: "What does his voice sound like?" "What games does she like best?" "Does he collect butterflies?" Reading college essays is when admissions officers are at their best - opening their hearts child-like to new experience; and they seek to know what is truly important to you and about you. All their number concerns are left elsewhere, in some big sack, as they read your essay. They are open to what you have to say.

By the time you have reached 16, 17, or 18, you really have something worthwhile to say. Sometimes you might not think so, sometimes even your parents might not think so, but you do. We ALL have stories to tell of course. And we all love to hear stories. So the college essay should tell a story, no more, no less. It should let the reader learn something about you that can't be learned elsewhere in the application. And it must show and not tell. That's what good stories do. They don't harangue. They tell a story and let the gentle reader draw the lessons about who is good or bad, and why. Good writing counts, but it's not the kind of writing you find in an English theme, contrasting Hawthorne and Melville. The writing should be as personal as a phone call. As warm as a letter from an old friend. It should be like a conversation, but with "ahs" and "likes" stricken. It should have color, detail, and texture; perhaps bits of dialogue, strong verbs, bright adjectives. Above all, it should be genuine: only you could have written that essay. You should hear your voice, as if you were chatting away with a friend sitting next to you on a long bus ride - chatting about real stories from real life. The essay can't be forced or phony. If you've read a hundred thousand college essays (as some college admissions officers have - like the two of us), you can spot the inauthentic. Fred Jewett, Dean of Admissions at Harvard decades back, said it best: "Things that are fake clank!" But words from the heart go to the heart. Such words are where your power lies. Yet another reason "to find the key that unlocks me."

Tell the college something that matters to you. The essay is the time to talk about what's important to you, whether it's about something big or something small. You don't need to have done something momentous to write a great college essay; you don't need to have spent your summers climbing Mt. Everest or writing the great American novel. That is not what's expected. The colleges expect you to have been up to exactly what you have been up to: developing your cognitive skills, so that you can arrive at the college and make use of what the academy can pass on to you, and developing your character and values, so that you can assimilate the experiences the college has to offer, both in and out of class. Colleges love stories from real life. Your life. That's what the colleges are after - your ideas, your observations, your take on things.

23

And isn't that a wonderful message: That the colleges actually care about your take on things? Think about it. Colleges have experiences to offer; what will your take be on them? Know this: In the rest of the world, college admissions is hung entirely on your performance on a national examination. That's the beginning and end of it (not just part of it, as here). Here in the US college admissions officers want to hear about what you truly care about.

TURNING THE KEY

Getting started. Take a crack at the resume and reflection process outlined below; it can help you find "the key that unlocks me," the key that nicely fits. Each person has one. Do the fun exercise too that follows this introduction. Be sure to look with your heart, not just your mind. And they'll be plenty of light to see. Never forget in your heart there is a lantern that can light the way.

The key that unlocks comes from an inward journey - pausing to see with the heart what is important to you. We feel strongly that you should always begin the college process by first developing a resume - a list of courses taken, grades earned, honors or awards received, extracurricular activities, summer experiences, travel experiences, work experiences. Such a resume is accumulated not in one fell swoop, but over a couple of weeks' time...on a pad of paper left openly out on the table at home, or as a Desktop document, so you can easily jot down things remembered. The resume should include everything you have been up to across your high school years, in and out of school.

Why do this? For two reasons. First, so that you can gaze upon the resume when done and realize the enormous distance you have traveled over these past three or four years, and feel a rightful, empowering sense of pride. And second, and even more important, so you can then reflect on what it all means. After all has been duly remembered and listed, you should take some quiet time to go off and reflect on your resume, on each and every item. This takes proper time, since we are all multifaceted. We are a lot like the amazing Phantom Tollbooth character that Milo meets when he arrives in Digitopolis, a strange mathematical land. Upon entering, Milo encounters a huge, phantasmagorical twelve-sided figure, the Dodecahedron, who slowly turns and twists, revealing one facet after another to Milo. He then glares down at the little boy in his little car and booms:

> *"Sides I have many,*
> *Angles not a few.*
> *I am the Dodecahedron,*
> *Who are you?"*

The Dodecahedron is like all of us, even at 17. We have a lot of facets and angles to our lives that need to be explored, to find out exactly who we are.

Here are the kinds of questions you should ask of your resume and yourself as you scrutinize it. Why have you chosen to be wet with the swim team for 17 hours a week for the past four years? Why did you take AP Biology or that fourth year of French? Why did you spend weekends for three years learning how to repair every kind of complex bike imaginable? Perhaps this resume and reflection process will tell you something, not only about skills you want to exercise and build upon in the future, but also something about your values. Maybe it will tell you some things about where you might be headed, how you want to occupy yourself during your college years, what kind of colleges might help you to attain your goals. The resume and reflection process can become the energizing force, the driving force, behind developing an appropriate set of college choices and the effective presentation of yourself to the colleges through the application, essay, and interview - since you will now arrive at these occasions with a story to tell. As you approach the essay and interview, instead of asking the wrong question - "What do they want to hear?" - you will ask the right question: "What do I want to tell them?" "What is it about me that I think they should know?" It will put you in the position to seize the initiative and to tell your story in your own best interest.

"It takes courage to grow up and become the person who you are," the poet e.e. cummings observed. Reaching for "the key that unlocks me" is a grand strategy to build confidence that you know, or know you can always find out, the answer to the question of who you are and who you are becoming. You do need to have courage to become the person who you are, as you best know it and as best you can. You also need the key that unlocks you.

A FINAL WORD. · *Beauty, yes*

Admissions officers don't expect perfection, although people often think they do. As admissions officers we'd see piles of recommendations coming in that seemed to suggest we were seeking "perfection." We could tell because they would begin as follows: "Heather is gem." "Jenny is a jewel." "Jonathon is a diamond-in-the-rough." (There was a whole gemology.) But college admissions officers don't expect perfection of themselves and they don't expect it of candidates for admission. Rather, they are interested in the real and the authentic, and in human beauty, the kind that can have the subtle elegant effects of human imperfection. Consider this insight from the great science essayist Chet Raymo:

The secret of gems is the secret of matter itself, which allows itself the privilege of geometrical connection; but the beauty of gems derives from more than geometrical order. Imperfections and impurities account for much of their beauty: the blue of sapphire, the green of emerald, the rainbow of tourmaline, the cat's eye of chrysoberyl, the star of star ruby are all explained by variations from perfection. Beauty, as perceived by the human mind, is derived from a delicate balance of order and chaos.

Beauty yes, perfection no. So know your college admissions readers just might adore your essay, whether the topic be large or small, on a stumble or a triumph, or something that combines both, as long it's an essay about something you truly care about. Good luck on your journey to find "the key that unlocks me" and good luck too in your college search.

Perfection, no

 A JOURNEY'S QUIZ

In order to find your own special key, try answering at least ten of these questions or prompts. Have fun. Answer the questions with great abandon. We know you will find that you are magical, magnificent, and mystical...

Who are your real-life heroes?

Qualities you value in your friends...

My dream job...

My greatest fear...

I care about...

I feel magical when I...

Proudest accomplishment...

My childhood dreams...

What's on your summer sound track?

First memory...

I am the happiest when...

Favorite gift...

Most treasured possession...

Perfect day...

Greatest regret...

What would you do on an impulse?

Favorite quote...

What is your idea of perfect happiness?

I never leave home without...

Favorite word...

I admire...

Greatest extravagance...

Favorite writers...

Favorite piece of art...

I dance with great abandon when...

What makes you angry?

It was like being in a movie when...

The hardest thing I ever had to do was...

The title of my autobiography...

I am courageous when...

I am magnificent when...

I daydream about...

Now that you have responded to these prompts, take some time to "connect the dots" between your responses here and your activities resume - this is the reflection part of the process. We promise you will find the key that unlocks your stories. You will have discovered essay topics that are core stories. If you have chosen the topics that are close to your heart, the story will spill out across the page in your own voice and will have power and authenticity.

We hope that the following essays written by other high school seniors applying to college will inspire you. And remember what the poet Rumi said, "Only from the heart can you touch the sky."

Essays from the hearts of boys

MY DOG'S NAME IS EINSTEIN

Every time I flip on a light switch, it reminds me of the beauty of the simple circuit. I first came across this electrical mystery as young boy experimenting with the odds and ends in my dad's toolbox. "Stay out of there, Jonathan; I don't want you getting hurt," he said, but along with my faithful dog, Einstein, I tinkered in his toolbox anyway. Two copper wires, a nine-volt battery, and a standard light bulb would "wow" me time after time. Each time that filament lit up I wanted to understand how and why it worked, and I let nothing get in my way.

As I grew older, I developed a passion for baseball. My love for science made its way onto the diamond where the same questions, "How?" and "Why?" followed everything. I began to think about the game from a scientific perspective. Why did a knuckleball flutter? How does an outfielder judge a fly ball? Why does a curveball curve? My mom found a gift that combined my love for science and baseball. She picked up the book that would instantly feed my hunger for knowledge and begin to answer my questions about the science of the game I loved. I struggled with the concepts at first, but The Physics of Baseball, by Robert Adair, became a book that fueled my interest in science.

When I began high school, my dad built a photography dark-room in our basement. I learned the finer aspects of the art of photography by feel, but questions about how and why still lingered. How does the camera capture the image? How do the chemicals, developer, stopper and fixer interact with the negatives? Why do shutter speed and aperture matter? By now I could research on my own and begin to evolve as a scientific thinker. My curiosity was insatiable.

What I have learned so far in my AP Environmental Science class makes me want to use my love for science to help the environment. Recently, I have become interested in issues regarding alternative fuel sources and clean water production for third world countries. Many ideas flood my mind about possible ways to solve the world's environmental problems with scientific reasoning.

I've always wondered "Why?" and "How?" All the questions I've asked before are questions I will continue to ask. I am on a quest for knowledge, and this quest has no end in sight - just ask Einstein.

I Hear America Singing

"I hear America singing, the varied carols I hear..."

--Walt Whitman

As long as I can recall I have been captivated by great American political voices: Washington, Lincoln, Roosevelt, and others who have used political speech to unite, heal, and inspire the American people.

The common thread that joins these men and women is their ability to hear the "varied carols" of the American people and to respond to their plight and pain with vigor, empathy, and a new vision of America, the other side of adversity. Washington heard the American people's cry for freedom and responded selflessly: "Our cruel and unrelenting enemy leaves us only the choice of brave resistance, or the most abject submission. We have, therefore, to resolve to conquer or die." He left his Presidency graciously, urging the American people ever on in their striving for freedom and the lasting attainment of a beloved country of their own.

Lincoln healed our nation in its time of its most dire distress - 650,000 Civil War soldiers dead, above and beyond civilian losses. While most in his government called for vengeance and retribution against the South, Lincoln provided a vision of a reunited America with simple, almost biblical cadences: "With malice towards none, with charity for all, with firmness in the right, as God gives us to see the right."

Dealing with a national despair unparalleled in our nation's history, Franklin Roosevelt provided a light of hope at the end of a tunnel of desolation: "This great Nation will endure as it has endured, will revive and will prosper... let me assert my firm belief that the only thing we have to fear is fear itself."

At crucial times in our history such leaders have not only elevated the spirits of our people, but have inspired the nation to achieve what few could even envision. In these times the true strength and character of our nation has become apparent, and our country's true greatness has become manifest.

I have been inspired not only by the quasi-mythical figures out of our nation's past, but also by figures closer to our time, those who have shown that a listening heart and a political voice can unite and even inspire - by John and Robert Kennedy who motivated their generation and had lasting impact on mine; by Martin Luther King Jr. who propelled people of all colors in ways revolutionary for his day; by Marian Wright Edelman who today reminds us that the future is not just ethereal thought, but that it must exist in the well being of our children.

My interest in political voice has particular relevance in our time, when civil discourse in American political life has deteriorated, and the political fabric itself seems frayed at the edges. Politicians seem compelled to undermine opponents through personal assaults and to belittle the ideas of others rather than inspire through their own ideas. I believe strongly that it is the duty of the next generation, my generation, as we head toward political maturity, to bring back the inspirational power of civil discourse and political voice that has sustained and lifted our nation. I also know that doing so begins not by speaking, but by listening carefully to

America's varied carols.

As I lie in my bed reading, after a long day of school, I actually wonder sometimes whose voices will remind us, as did Robert Kennedy's, that "Each time a man stands up for an ideal, or acts to improve the lot of others, or strikes out against injustice, he sends forth a tiny ripple of hope, and crossing each other, from a million different centers of energy and daring, those ripples build a current which can sweep down the mightiest walls of oppression and resistance...." I hope and believe that the people of my generation will once again use the political stage to offer voices of hope and guidance to a people in need.

THE PHYSICS OF RACING

As the first corner approached, a long high speed sweeper taken at full throttle, an impulse of panic gripped my soul. Was fate about to deal me a visit to the outside retaining wall, or was my car going to stay on the black stuff and reward me with a fast lap time for driving on the edge? The front tires gripped the surface like an octopus's suction cups grappling onto its prey. The rear end snapped violently and suddenly out of control. The car careened into the barrier with a loud crack that reverberated like a pistol shot in a cavern. The track marshals raced to the scene of the wreck, but they had no need to scoop my remains from the cramped cockpit. I was standing 20 yards away, piloting my 1/12th scale Speedmerchant Rev. 3 by radio control.

I had spent the two days before the 2002 Electric Asphalt Nationals in Denver attempting, to no avail, to find the perfect weight distribution that would permit the highest cornering speed while still keeping my hotrod from spinning out. Instead of gliding around the course as if on rails, the racer fought me like a 400-pound drunk clinging to his barstool at closing time. With the fury of a hurricane bearing down on the Florida coast, I hefted the miniature machine, contemplated hurling it against the wall, and then realized that the fault lay not with the $1000 "paper weight," but with the driver, me.

Although no trophy engraved with both my name and "national champion" adorned my room, I had gained something much more valuable: experience. I realized that I would have a better chance of making a profit in Vegas than showing up at a big race and expecting to do well without sufficient practice, preparation, and knowledge. To succeed, I would need to learn how to properly set up the car, which required analyzing the physics of racing.

With the help of Bruce Carbone, a veteran of radio controlled racing and Mr. Pierson, my physics teacher, I looked into the chief principles of power and handling. My brain buzzed concepts that I had never before considered: suspension geometry, dampening forces, tire compound and construction, as well as surface friction, electronic and electromagnetic impulses.

Six months of pouring over the books and tinkering at the workbench finally resulted in a car I could understand and one I believed would dominate the track. Instead of socializing with my friends, staying up late talking on AOL or going out to movies and parties, I spent my leisure time at the track practicing. My lap times decreased with every pass of the finish line. I accelerated past my competition at the local level and zoomed to the Regionals where I positioned myself for a slot at the 2003 Electric Asphalt Nationals in Raleigh.

At the Nationals I took advantage of every practice session. Seeking the ideal set up for that track. After a blistering qualifying run my car positioned itself towards the front of the field. However, not wanting to risk damage to my highly tuned vehicle, I skipped the morning warm-up the day of the race itself. Figuring that the track had not changed much over the previous few days, I rationalized, why should it change overnight? But fate dealt me a hard blow. Unbeknownst to me, it had rained while I slept in late the morning of the race. A shower had completely drenched the track, leaving the surface with a coefficient of friction lower than that of a watery ice rink.

When the starting tone went off, I yanked the accelerator. The machine leaped far ahead on the opening straightaway. Filled with confidence that rivaled the hubris of Oedipus, I waited to the last second to slam on the brakes in the turn. To my horror the tires locked up and my hotrod slid across the asphalt into the side of my nearest competitor. Parts flew at every direction as I watched an entire year of hard work break up into bits. Lesson learned: The price of victory is eternal vigilance.

Phillips Screwdrivers, Hex Keys, Tire Levers

Phillips screwdrivers, hex keys, tire levers - these are some of my most valuable possessions. I love the clatter of tools, the grease on my arms and hands, and even the smell of the citrus degreaser I use to clean up at the end of a work day. I don't even mind the scuffed knuckles. I love being surrounded by flat tires, bent wheels, and the mangled bikes run over by cars that are hauled daily into Frank's Spoke 'N' Wheel, the shop where I've worked now for four years. I am a mechanical kind of guy. Since I was little, I've instinctively known how to fix almost anything. My older brother worked at Frank's, and so as soon as I turned fourteen, I jumped at the chance to work along side him. Not only was I proud of landing my first job, it was also a chance to work with older guys from my neighborhood. First, I started by building brand-new bikes - straight out of the boxes. The very first bike that I ever built was a kid's bike. It was a red and black Gary Fisher Tyro. Because it was the first bike I ever built, I remember how excited I was when the five-year-old arrived with his dad to pick it up. Since then, I have graduated from "tike bikes" to 2500 dollar Lemond road bikes.

Now I have regular customers who actually count on me, especially at the busiest time of the year, early August, as bikers from all over Massachusetts state prepare for the oldest, largest, most successful charity bike ride in the country - The Pan Mass Challenge. On any given day, I repair at least eight bikes, getting them ready to be ridden 200 miles in two days from Sturbridge in Central Massachusetts to Provincetown at the very tip of Cape Cod. The riders work very hard for a long time to get ready, and so I want to be sure that their ride will be breakdown free. Many hundreds of thousands of dollars are raised for cancer through the Pan Mass, and I am glad to be a part of a wonderful event. It is a chance to combine my love of the mechanical and my involvement in community service, two of my top out of class involvements.

We Live in Hamilton's Country

"There is an elegant memorial in Washington to Jefferson, but none to Hamilton. However, if you seek Hamilton's monument, look around. You are living in it. We honor Jefferson, but live in Hamilton's country..."

--*Henry Cabot Lodge*

It is the Fourth of July, and I am in Washington, the nation's beautiful and awe inspiring capital. It is the southern city that Thomas Jefferson and James Madison wished for, loaded with monuments to our nation's great leaders. My thoughts though are not with these men, but with the man who made Jefferson's wish possible. Alexander Hamilton of New York made possible Jefferson's desire to locate our capital next to his beloved Virginia, as he made possible so much in the way we live our lives in the United States and how we govern ourselves. How peculiar then that looking for a marble monument to Hamilton is an exercise in futility. In fact, other than realizing every once in a while that he is on the ten-dollar bill, few Americans think much about him. Perhaps this is what first fascinated me about Hamilton two years ago. The more I learned as I went through my APUSH class at Wayland HS, the more interested I became in this man, generally ignored or even reviled, as the "anti-Jefferson" by most Americans, yet perhaps more responsible for our nation's economic success than any of our more famous founders. I am here to study AP US Government with the Junior Statesmen of America, and so today, on our country's birthday, I decided to write my college essay about someone who is truly a hero in the creation of our great democracy.

What do you say about someone who distinguished himself in the Revolutionary War, wrote two thirds of the Federalist Papers, was the first Secretary of the Treasury, and created the national bank and financial system that he knew the new nation needed to create wealth and political stability? (He did the last by compromising with Jefferson, placing the capital in the South and gaining passage of his financial plan.) It was Hamilton's economic vision that made it possible for many of our people, though still not all, to have a decent economic life. If you think about the famous words on the Statue of Liberty, "Give us your tired, your poor, your huddled masses, yearning to be free," many generations of immigrants came to the US for economic betterment, political and religious freedom, and political stability. In many ways we have all these because of Hamilton.

What are the qualities in him I admire? Born in the West Indies, he found himself impoverished, with his father abandoning his family and his mother dying when Alexander was only eleven. He went to live with relatives and, through his own brilliance, self-education, and drive he was running a mercantile business by the age of thirteen, and in two different languages, English and French. Realizing he was a genius some older friends pooled their funds to send him to America, where, at sixteen, he entered what is now Columbia University. By eighteen he was already writing highly influential revolutionary pamphlets. He became a passionate nationalist, and in the American Revolution a close aide of General Washington. Washington continued to rely upon Hamilton's vision across the years, such that Hamilton wrote most of Washington's Farewell Address, which is still revered for its wisdom. When the Articles of Confederation were proving unworkable, it was Hamilton's influence that caused the calling of the Constitutional Convention. He wanted a very strong central government, but even when he failed to win certain features, he still brought his powers of persuasion to the writing of the Federalist Papers, a huge factor in gaining ratification of the Constitution. Even today, when the Supreme Court debates great constitutional questions, they always go back to the Federalist Papers. What is it about Hamilton that I admire? His economic vision, his willingness to offer political compromise to achieve greater goals, and his willingness to present a "unity platform" after failing to achieve his own goals at the Constitutional Convention. He was able to achieve all he did through grit, hard work, drive, self study, courage, and daring. When people think of Emma Lazarus's words on the Statue of Liberty, they should think too of Hamilton, along with Jefferson, Adams, and Madison.

It is curious that Hamilton's contributions are not more recognized in the country that, as Lodge says, is "his monument." I have not found a good explanation for it. Was it because he was killed in a duel with Aaron Burr who was something of a despicable character? Does his death in a duel, by a custom thankfully out of fashion today, somehow diminish him in the eyes of Americans?

I have been particularly interested in the founding of our country. Certainly much is owed to the pen of Jefferson, the integrity of Washington, and the persistence of Adams. But personally, I have the greatest admiration for the person who was most responsible for making it all work: Alexander Hamilton. After all, we do "live in Hamilton's country."

SPIDER WEBS CAN HOLD DOWN A LION

While the majority of dreams are so fleeting or trivial,

they are seldom remembered; still others can change

the dreamer - or sometimes the world. There are spec-

tacular examples of inspirational messages inscribed

in dream, where one awakens to a wholly new vision.

Dr. Frederick Banting desperately sought a diabetes

drug to help relieve suffering, and his revelation of

how-to came, not in a lab, but in a dream (and later

won him a Nobel Prize). In 1963, on the steps of the

Lincoln Memorial, with hundreds of thousands gath-

ered round, Martin Luther King delivered his "I Have

a Dream" speech; it altered our nation's history by gal-

vanizing supporters of desegregation, which led to en-

actment of the 1964 Civil Rights Act.

I too have a dream; to be precise, it's one I heard of and adopted as my own. I stand before Three Doors, each leading to a packed banquet hall. Behind Door One, all guests consume bountiful foods spread before them; the scene one of gratification and joy. Behind Door Two - the Middle Door - is chaos and cacophony, a scene as if from a farcical Marx Brothers' film. Each diner has an immobilizing board strapped to each arm, making it impossible to bend even a wrist or an elbow. Each diner's attempt to pick up food is followed by plates falling and food flying through the air - not a morsel reaching a diner. There was starvation amid plenty. Behind Door Three, the scene, while similar, was different in consequence. Each diner likewise had arms stiffened and immobilized with splint-like contraptions, yet all were well fed and happy. Each diner simply lifted a plate and turned to the right, with outstretched stiffened arms, to offer food to a needy neighbor. They had learned to feed each other. The lesson? We either think of the whole community or we "starve" as individuals.

I became involved in community service gradually, and then far more deeply, but first through Peer Helpers. I began tutoring students in math, a personal academic strength; these were students who might better understand how to solve a math problem with an assist from a schoolmate. I then began to take part in one-on-one basketball mentoring clinics. Soon, I started to raise funds for "Basketball Shoot-outs" for kids with disabilities - kids who sometimes feel they don't even "deserve" to be on a basketball court; children who might never experience the joy of the "swish," which I do (on a good day!). Why can't a child in a wheel chair experience the same sound as I do, in a game I love? Almost always, a child's "conquering" a math problem, or a child's taking a shot through the orange rim, is followed by a child's smile. I want to make it clear: I don't do this selflessly. I do it because it is fun. The great humanitarian, Dr. Albert Schweitzer, said, "The only ones among you who will be truly happy are those who have sought, and found, how to serve."

Sponsored by the Boston Celtics, in conjunction with Easter Seals, I raised over $20,000 for Basketball Shoot-outs in the past seven years. Easter Seals named me Outstanding Youth Volunteer in 2003 and recently I was recognized at the Massachusetts State House as "A Hero Among Us" - someone who has had "an overwhelming impact on the lives of others through humanitarian spirit and lasting contributions to community." I was also honored at a Boston Celtics game with the cheers and applause of 18,000 people ringing in my ears.

Yet, I find it odd that I, an able-bodied person, was designated "A Hero Among Us." To me real heroes are disabled children and their parents who sacrifice everything to fight for life, health, respect, inclusion, and things that other people blindly take for granted. Recently, I saw first hand what "A Hero Among Us" truly is, for we had one in our home - and it wasn't me. My father courageously battled cancer, never missing a day of work or backing away from a responsibility. I am no hero. I am one among you, seeking others. Change comes, not from one person's efforts, but from a community's action. I think of the African Proverb, first heard on the continent where, I've learned from history, human community was invented: "Spider-webs, when woven together, can hold down a lion."

Third Grade Football

"If Jeff doesn't play, then I don't play." The words had popped out of my mouth before I had a chance to think about them. Now, as I looked from face to face, it dawned on me that I was jeopardizing my own position for someone with whom I wasn't even friends. I felt myself wavering, but one glance at Jeff's expression of renewed hope made up my mind. I looked at the captain of my team and he must have sensed my determination, because he shrugged his shoulders and said "Okay, Jeff's with us." With that, the daily third grade recess football match got under way.

I didn't think much more about the incident until my Mom got a phone call later that evening from Jeff's mom. Jeff had come home smiling that day for the first time in weeks, as his severe dyslexia and worsening stutter were making him increasingly withdrawn at school. Being included in the football game with the "cool" kids had meant the world to him. My parents told me that they had never been so proud of me and that what I had done meant more to them than any goal I could score or homerun I could hit. Frankly, I didn't know what the big deal was, and I quickly forgot about the event.

Years later at the end of my freshman year a lot of kids began urging me to run for class president. Everyone had thought that the class president had done a poor job for the year, and elections for sophomore year were just around the corner. Secretly I had always wanted to run for class president, but I worried about whether I would be able to do the good job that the class deserved. Being President required a staggering amount of time and I just was not sure that I had it with all of the other extracurricular activities I had on my plate. In the end, I gave in and put my name in as a candidate for president.

My timing could not have been worse, for the week of campaigning coincided with the same week as the playoffs for baseball, not to mention that I was absolutely swamped with schoolwork. I knew that I would not be able to make all the signs and everything necessary for the campaigns. The night before the campaign began I went to bed exhausted from baseball practice and schoolwork. I drifted off to sleep worried about what tomorrow would bring.

As my dad and I pulled within view of the school the next morning my heart dropped, there were already people outside campaigning. Immediately, I felt regret for having put in my name as a candidate. As we got closer though, I saw the signs and a majority of them said "VOTE JOHN GALVIN." I could not believe it, where had all these signs come from? As I walked into school and looked around, the halls were also covered with signs saying "VOTE JOHN GALVIN." I stood stunned for a minute, not knowing what to say or do. Feeling someone standing beside me, I looked over and there was Jeff. "How'dya like the signs?" he asked. I told him how shocked I was and asked if he knew where they came from. He laughed and said he had been waiting to pay me back all these years and finally found a way to do it. When I said there was no way he did it himself, he told me that he had just gotten other kids who I had treated the same way to help. I was lost for words, but he just smiled and punched me in the arm.

Bury My Heart Not My Mind

For the most part my parents dealt patiently with my incessant questioning. They assumed it was just a phase that I would outgrow. My teachers, however, loved the fact that I wanted to know more about the why and how of every subject that came up. Mrs. Busconi, my second grade teacher, spent an entire mid-year conference raving about my inquisitive mind. My parents just looked at each other and rolled their eyes.

As I grew older, my "questioning phase" raged on. History proved to be an especially ripe topic that seemed to beg my inquiries, that is, until an encounter with my eighth grade social studies teacher, Mr. Vessa. Perhaps he was having a bad day, or maybe he was just sick of my questions; but one day while I was querying him as to whether Thomas Jefferson was really an abolitionist, given the fact that he had had over one hundred fifty slaves, he looked at me in annoyance and said, "John, look at your textbook, page 245. It says that Thomas Jefferson was an abolitionist. If Thomas Jefferson wasn't an abolitionist it wouldn't be in the textbook!"

From that point on I stifled my questions, although at times it was very hard to do. When we got to the chapter on Manifest Destiny and the Trail of Tears, my head swirled with confusion. How could our government have forced thousands of Cherokees on a journey to nowhere in the middle of winter? Who decided that the white race was so superior that it could trample on all others in pursuit of its dreams? Still stinging from Mr. Vessa's earlier rebuke, I repressed my suspicion that an important part of the story was missing from my textbook.

For the next two years I continued to squelch my questioning tendencies. I did not think much about the Native Americans either, until the summer before my junior year, when I delved into my AP U.S. History summer reading list. With two weeks left before school opened, I began the eighth and final book, Dee Brown's *Bury My Heart at Wounded Knee – An Indian History of the American West*. At first I just wanted to get it over with, but as I read on I found myself embroiled in the story. My sense of outrage and shame grew with each ensuing chapter until it became so painful that I wanted to put the book down, but found that I couldn't. I discovered that the white man, in his unrelenting quest for enrichment and glory, had destroyed the culture, pride and livelihood of an entire race. How could this have happened? The personal accounts of Native Americans revealed a culture whose philosophy of life, kinship with nature, and innate sense of dignity made a mockery of those who labeled them savages. In comparison, the greed, dishonesty and cruelty of the white man begs the question of whether or not it was they who should be called savages. As I struggled to sort through my swirling emotions, a Nez Percés chief, Yellow Wolf, helped to clarify my thoughts in his statement, "The whites told only one side. Told it to please themselves. Told much that is not true. Only his own best deeds, only the worst deeds of the Indians, has the white man told." Yellow Wolf could have been talking about my textbook. It tells only one side of the story, the white side, and this does us a great disservice. We study history so that we can learn from the mistakes of our past in order to avoid repeating them. Looking around at the world today, it is obvious that our lessons have not been learned. Our country is still trying to impose our values on people of other cultures. Our leaders are still too willing to put the interests of the rich and powerful ahead of the needs of the less fortunate.

Yellow Wolf helped me realize that a textbook, like any other form of media, could reflect the bias of its authors and thus influence the reader's understanding of an issue. Never again will I unquestioningly accept conventional wisdom. Thanks to Dee Brown I now know that challenging what I am taught is the only way to arrive at my own version of the truth.

Spirit in the Sky

On the day of the race, the sky was calm and the morning sun glowed brightly, warming the cool arid Colorado air. "Perfect race conditions," another runner was saying. I was wearing a pair of RaceReady running shorts stuffed with four Gu energy gels, a Dri-Fit Nike shirt, a lightweight windbraker, my favorite Boston Red Sox hat, and my venerable Nike running shoes. There were five others in my group about to run the Pike's Peak Ascent Mountain Race: my father, my brother John, my friend Robby and his father, and our family friend Bob Shultz. I was quivering with a blend of excitement and anxiety. The mountain was barely visible and had an ominous presence, seemingly reaching as far and as high as the heavens. Even with all my training and equipment, I was not prepared for what was to come.

I knew that the Pike's Peak ascent was going to challenge my physical and mental endurance, so my father, brother and I devised a lengthy training regimen for the summer: a combination of running up local mountains and lengthy treadmill workouts. Mt. Monadnock, double Mt. Wachusetts, and Mt. Washington runs were commonplace for us. Every weekend we piled into the minivan and drove off to conquer another mountain. Mt. Monadnock was our first victim; its rock and root riddled terrain gave us a little trouble at first, but its 3,165 foot peak gradually came within grasp. Mt. Wachusetts was the next in our lineup, and its 2,006 foot summit seemed as if it would be a cinch, until Robby's father came up with the brilliant notion to run a double, traversing up and down the trails twice! It was mind numbing to realize that when I reached the bottom I would only be half done. We also used the opportunity of the Mt. Washington Road Race to train for Pike's Peak, a 14,110 foot high mountain, and returned several times to run up the forest trails. In addition to these mountain excursions we trained on the treadmill. These workouts consisted of running three to eight miles with the treadmill set at two-thousand to six-thousand vertical feet of elevation change. To escape the boredom and monotony of running in the same place for up to three hours at a time, we rented movies and books on tape.

Racing up Pike's Peak, the sound of labored breathing and quiet footfalls permeated the cold mountain air. Hundreds of racers moved up the long switchbacks, creating what looked like a giant snake, slowly slithering up to the peak to claim its throne. The rest stops were a blessing, as cheering fans provided emotional support, plenty of Gatorade to help replenish our dehydrated bodies, and chairs for us to rest in. However, these chairs were also considered a curse, as one experienced runner told me, "No matter how tired

you get, never sit down. If you sit down you won't stand up again."
I repeated this mantra whenever I passed a rest station and, placing
one foot in front of the other, I continued up the mountain.

Every step of the last three miles of Pike's Peak was an ago-
nizing battle; the oxygen was much thinner and running became
impossible. To make matters worse, a torrent of hail pelted me for
hours; large pebble sized chunks of ice, whizzed through the chill-
ing air, stinging my exhausted body. As we got higher and higher
the conditions got worse and worse; a full fledged thunderstorm
was brewing in the sky and bright violet bolts of searing lightning
were exploding in the sky. An abandoned radio was lying 20 feet
off the side of the path, loudly playing Spirit in the Sky. I looked
up to gauge my progress, and there they were, the famous sixteen
golden steps. I was surprised to find that they were not steps at all,
but a quick succession of sixteen switchbacks leading to the finish
line.

The mountain had done everything in its power to keep me
from reaching the summit. It tried to freeze my legs and thin the air
to stop my movement, it tried to scare me away with cacophonous
bursts of thunder, and finally it attacked me with a furious barrage
of hail. But I had made it; and as I crossed the finish line I thrust my
hands into the air and said, "This one's for you, Uncle Mark!" Mark
was my father's brother, who died after a three year battle with a
rare form of germ cell cancer in December, 2002. He was dedicated
to making life easier for the ones he cared about. When I was learning how to write, schoolmates would tease me about being the
only left handed person. Uncle Mark convinced me that being left
handed was not a curse -- for he too was left handed. He would
always tell me that instead of microwaving a snack for ten seconds
microwave it for eleven, because punching in 11 is easier and faster
than punching in 10. Dr. Vikas Sukhatme, who I had the privilege
of interning for, was the doctor who suggested that Uncle Mark

take anti-angiogenesis drugs to prolong his life, and although it was not enough so save him, Mark was comforted by knowing that a team of intelligent doctors were doing their best to find a cure.

The summit was covered in a six inch blanket of hail chunks, growing thicker and thicker over the past two hours. It felt as if I had been racing for six month, and the weather seemed to agree. I was hungry, wet, and exhausted, but most of all relieved; that the race was over and that I had succeeded. Minutes after I crossed the finish line, the hail ceased, the clouds dispersed, and rays of bright sunshine filtered through the clouds, warming the frozen ground. It was as if a magnanimous spirit had acknowledged our accomplishment and allowed us to recover in peace. However, chaos and weariness still reigned on that mountain summit; shuttles could not take down enervated runners because the roads were too icy. The medical tent and gift shop quickly filled to the brim, bursting with shivering bodies attempting to warm themselves, while many more waited outside for the shuttles to finally get clearance to take them home. Someone said, "We can walk down to the parking lot, its only three miles." I thought he was crazy! As it became clear that we would be waiting a long, long, long time, I was surprised to hear a voice say, "Lets do it." It was my own.

I not only reached the summit of Pike's Peak that day, breaking all personal records and coming to realize just how far I could push myself, but I also felt like I had done something significant in Uncle Mark's memory, by running in his honor and by participating in an event that raised $25,000 for cancer research.

D U E L

"*Strike!*" *I look out at the pitcher, Jimmy Thorndike,*
and smile. "*Three and one count and you throw a*
curve," I think. "*Jimmy, you've got some guts. I'll let*
you have that one."

I step out of the batter's box and look around. It seems as
though most of the school has turned out for the biggest game of
the season against our archrival, Dover-Sherborn. As I take my routine practice swing I think to myself, "He just threw me a curve ball,
does he have it in him to throw one again?" I decide he doesn't.
With his team up by two in the last inning and men on first and
second he cannot afford to put the game-winning run on base by
walking me. He can't risk a changeup either, knowing that the last
time I faced him I had belted the changeup into the left-center gap
for a triple. Nope, Jimmy is going to come in with his fastball, and
with two outs and the game on the line, I figure the adrenaline he
has pumping through his body will leave the pitch just a little high.
I visualize myself smashing his high heat into the gap in right. With
this vision in mind, I step into the box and go through my warm
up routine.

This is why I love baseball. There is no other team sport in
which you can have a one-on-one duel going on in the middle
of an eighteen player field, a duel that is as much mental as it is

physical as the pitcher and batter try to outthink each other. The pressure can be enormous as all eyes focus on just two players: the pitcher trying to hurl a ball at eighty or more miles per hour through a small imaginary strike zone, and the batter who is trying to hit that small speeding ball squarely with little more than a stick. Mastering skills like throwing and catching and hitting can only take you so far. To really excel at the game you have to be relaxed and focused enough to block out all else besides the duel occurring between you and the pitcher. I thrive on this kind of pressure. While others like Jimmy worry about the outcome, I focus on what pitch is going to come next, and what I am going to do with it. Nothing else matters at the moment.

My warm up routine is over and I see Jimmy take the sign. The pitch comes in and sure enough, it's a fastball just above my belt. As I step into the pitch I hear the beautiful ping that only the sweet spot of a bat can make. Trotting toward first base, I watch the ball get smaller and smaller until it finally drops forty feet beyond the right field fence.

Is it a Good Day for Flying?

"Science, freedom, beauty, adventure...
Aviation offers it all."

--*Charles Lindbergh*

When I discover that it is the day, the questions race through my mind. Is it a good day for flying? What if something goes wrong? As the blue and white Cessna taxis out to the runway at Hanscom Field, my thoughts are focused on the airspace above. Breathe, I tell myself. You are ready. I steady myself by remembering that this is the result of months of hard work, and I am determined to press on. Still, anxiety, ordinary for all kinds of firsts, builds for this extraordinary one.

There is no feeling like the moment a pilot takes off, be it for the first time or the fiftieth. The romance of flight is not a myth. It is a mixture of apprehension, freedom, fulfillment, and especially adventure that I feel every week (weather permitting) while learning to fly. The sensations are amplified when I go up alone but were never more so than my first solo.

My thoughts flash back to my uncle, who took me for my first flight. Once a pilot for the Navy, he piqued my interest in aviation as soon as we took off. Seeing the earth stretch out below me made it seem like a whole other world that flight could unlock. In the air, all seemed at peace, and I felt I could journey to far-away lands that I yearned to explore. Other countries and other worlds seemed closer, more within reach, and my love of travel surged. Flight offered new places, new sights, and new opportunities.

Returning from my reverie, I hear the magic words, "cleared for takeoff," and maneuver into position. Now is no time to be nervous. I push in the throttle and pull back the yoke. In seconds, I am free of the ground, seemingly defying gravity. It hits me now – I am soloing. I am above the trees and among the clouds in the troposphere. I am practically in the weather, and it brings my interest in meteorology to life. The clockwise winds of an air mass are coming up against the plane just as they do a cumulus cloud. The airport buildings and runways fade into the distance, giving way to quaint town centers, sparkling blue lakes, and vast dense forests.

Other, more gratifying, emotions come flooding in, pushing concern aside. Soaring through the air alone is a thrill that only a relative few have experienced. As the world below me shrinks, I am filled with a proud sense of accomplishment in my feat. I have followed in the exclusive footprints (or vapor trails) of other aviators. I feel that I know the exhilaration of Amelia Earhart, Charles Lindbergh, and, of course, Orville and Wilbur Wright during their pioneering flights.

In the observation of Leonardo da Vinci, "Once you have tasted flight, you will forever walk the earth with your eyes turned skyward, for there you have been, and there you will always long to return." Now, when I hear airplanes roar above, I can count myself as one who has made that same journey into the blue.

DEBATING WITH DAD

The extracurricular activity in which I was most engaged -
debating - helped shape my interests in public policy.
--Joseph E. Stiglitz

Looking around this slightly dingy Indian restaurant one would not have thought this would be a place where intellectual fire could roar to the forefront of any conversation. In fact, it was hard to even concentrate as the smell of aromatic herbs and spices wafted throughout the small, cramped dining room. Waiters moved nimbly through the small tables carrying plates awash with colour. This was not your typical debating hall layered in dark wood with high ceilings and awash with intellectual presumptuousness. It was just a small restaurant, but for me, a traditional spot for debating with dad.

While waiting for our order, an unusual question suddenly started to blossom in my mind - not an unusual habit though, as I often catch myself thinking about issues related to policy and international relations. Sitting opposite from Dad, I started to wonder if charity was in essence always a good idea. At face value, it was, of course, a silly question to which the answer is obviously "yes". However, once I started to think about it, an argument soon emerged. Dad, sitting opposite me, broke his silence, "So what are you thinking?" I wasn't exactly sure what to say at first because in this day and age even mentioning that charity might not be a good thing could be considered misguided, heartless and lacking in empathy. But it was Dad I was sitting across from, so I knew he would not be too judgemental. I dared to propose my argument.

"So Dad, don't you think in some situations charity can be a bad thing?" I said as our starter arrived. "Why do you think that, and when would it be bad a thing?" Dad replied in a slightly bemused manner. He was used to my asking some odd and slightly provocative questions, but this one certainly caught him by surprise. I proceeded to go through an example. I brought up the fact that the European Union massively overproduces food because of the Common Agricultural Policy. The EU then "generously" donates the excess food to impoverished nations. It seems as though these wealthier nations are helping other less fortunate nations, but this is not the case when you consider the implications of the EU actions. The food donated to these nations depresses food prices as few individuals are willing to pay for food when they can get it for free. These actions drive the farmers out of business and the economies of the impoverished nations suffer. Ironically, the actions of the wealthier nations are often considered to be charity. My final point to Dad was that it might be better to remove tariffs on agricultural imports to the richer nations and allow free trade. After I presented my line of argument, we continued the debate, discussing the pros and cons of charity in this context.

Debating has been a natural part of family exchanges; once you start debating, you make it part of your daily experience. I feel that by debating issues, I challenge my own beliefs, keep an open mind, remain curious and search for new perspectives. I have my debating partner, Dad, to thank for that!

IN SEARCH OF ÉLAN BEYOND THE MATH

It isn't a new idea that numbers have countless uses. Over the years, I have used numbers in class for academic pursuits, in Math Team competitions, and certainly in daily life. Calculating tips, analyzing political polls, and figuring out a term grade are all practical applications for math, but they lack a certain spark. Math comes easily and satisfyingly to me, but a truly human connection is lacking in mere "plugging and chugging." However, one summer, I got the chance to apply math practically and for fun. As a big baseball fan, I was thrilled to invent and fill the unique position of statistician and scorekeeper with the local Red Sox Little League team for one season.

Of course, I enjoyed my actual task of scoring. I kept track of scores and at-bats for each game so that I could calculate every necessary stat, from a player's batting average to where he was most likely to hit the ball. My data were very valuable to the coaches, who were able to make lineup changes and position decisions based on my work. The kids were also curious about my statistics, so I began to share my information with them as well. As a result, they too appreciated the value of numbers outside the classroom. Pitchers knew when they were most effective from their earned run averages, and hitters could tell when they needed to make adjustments from their on base percentages. Slugging percentages told the team and me who hit the most home runs, and errors and assists spoke to defensive abilities. As our wins piled up, I liked to think that my stats were improving our game.

The season quickly became special for reasons that were not entirely mathematical. Through the months of summer, I went from not knowing most of the players to being very friendly with all of them. The camaraderie of the younger kids and the passion and dedication they had for baseball and one another added a new dimension to my task. It struck me how every player contributed to the team, both on the field and off. Shier players became more talkative over time as they became comfortable, so even they fit in, and the team cheered wildly every time one of the lesser batters made a good hit. Finally, the work of the season paid off when I shared in the excitement as our Red Sox won the town championship. I had gained a much richer experience than the world of statistics had promised at the beginning of the season. With my data, I was able to contribute a valuable element to the play of these young boys of summer, and they gave back to me with a less tangible reward: the spark of mathematics beyond mere numbers.

The Ghost In the Attic

My camera is loaded as I begin to look around, a million things flood my mind. I salivate at the possibilities. Light, shadow, patterns, angles, textures, emotions, actions, the promises are endless. It was late afternoon and I felt abandoned and alone amongst the old brick buildings and stonewalls. The campus was desolate as I made my way to my favorite place, the photo studio, to visit my photography teacher. She recommended I "burn a roll" of film at the school's chapel. "Don't be afraid to check out the whole chapel." She said, "Be careful, though." This struck me as a peculiar thing to say. She had taught here for over thirty years, did she know something about the rumors on campus? Was there really a "ghost" in the chapel attic?

A thin layer of snow covered the ground in places and icicles dripped from every tree branch. The sun broke through the thin clouds and its heat felt good on the back of my neck. Armed with my ancient Pentax K-1000 camera, I set out on a quest to capture the beast heard of only in campus stories and folk tales. I circled the old white chapel, whose paint was peeling from all sides. Entering the sacred place, I walked slowly up the staircase to the second floor benches where something caught my eye. Behind a stack of folding chairs, a small curved door hugged the far corner. What intrigued me was the handle on the door, for it wasn't a typical handle, but a latch like those on picket fences. There were only two shots left in my camera and I wanted to get something good.

I opened the door and crept up the rickety wooden staircase, when I felt a chill. To my right was a pile of old class pictures, stained yellow from years of abandonment. Across the way, sunbeams caught my eye and I spotted a lone window staring back at me. Had this been what my teacher had hinted about? The window was stained with water residue, dirt and dust and it seemed as if no one had been up here in decades. The iron rod holding the six sections of glass together was chipped and rusted and I wanted to pick at it with my fingernail, but feared the window would shatter if I did. A single fly lay lifeless against the window, a lonely black dot on a glowing sheet of glass. A thick woven rope sagged, looking exhausted in front of the window. The sun's natural light caught the rope in such a way as to highlight every single fiber.

I quickly drew my camera from its leather case and dropped to one knee to steady my shot. Adjusting the settings before the moment changed, I snapped off my last two frames. Scuttling down the stairs, I left the chapel and rushed across campus to the darkroom. Pulling the negatives from their final bath, the last one caught my eye. The ghost stared back at me and I couldn't wait to make a print, for the camera had captured for eternity what my eyes had seen for only a moment. I may not have captured the "ghost" of campus rumor, but my photography teacher was right. She always said, "photography makes the extraordinary out of the ordinary." This ghost now lives in my photo album.

STEVIE WONDER
NEVER CALLS IN SICK*

We sat down with Josh and discovered how he went from being that kid who you'll see on stage to being that kid on stage [and everything in between].

First question's easy. How'd it all start?

"Well, on Sunday mornings I would wake up and walk downstairs and hear my dad playing one of his CDs from this massive collection of more than 2,000. Usually some Ray Charles or the Beatles. Back then I didn't really care for it; it was just noise in the background. But I've realized that my father's persistent love of music was a lot more contagious than I could have predicted. So that was dad. Ms. Toland taught me trumpet out of one of those *Standard of Excellence* beginner books in fourth grade - she taught me in some form every year until she was my AP Music Theory teacher junior year. Now I devote about twenty hours to music-related activities in an average week. And if only there were more hours in the day, that number would be much higher."

Where does Wind Ensemble fit into the equation?

"Wind Ensemble is where I have finished what I started in the *Standard of Excellence* books. As I grew tremendously in my trumpet skills (making prestigious graduations from the amateur red book to the more advanced [for a six grader, of course] blue book and green book) to where I now sit, as one of the top three trumpet players at Weston High, I realized how much I loved not only trumpet, but music as a whole. After a while though, it dawned on me that perhaps I needed something else to relieve some persistently bottled-up creativity. Something with a little more . . . flavor."

And Jazz Band?

"With Jazz Band, suddenly life allowed some improvisation. Beginner arrangements of unknown classical overtures were replaced by tasteful and familiar tunes. I can still remember looking out at the audience to where the judges sat at our performance in May 2006. We were about halfway through *Flip, Flop & Fly* when my big improv solo moment came. I horrendously cracked the last note of my big finish, but it still felt unbelievable. This feeling of musical freedom for eight measures of music - eight measures of blank canvas. Eight measures of transcript paper that I could write on and scribble on and erase and add and change a million times. The crack wasn't part of the initial plan. But the passion behind it, well, that was penciled in the whole time. I played in Jazz Band every year of high school, ultimately doubling as a trumpet player and vocalist, further exploring the color and taste behind this new idea of real music."

Word on the street says your voice is the real strength, not your horn. How and when did you realize this?

"Well, I didn't join chorus until my first year of high school. Suddenly my musicianship was not restricted to fingerings and I learned blues scales - almost anything my imagination could conjure could be produced. And once I was accepted to the school's audition-only Concert Choir prior to my sophomore year, I was able to experience an even higher level of musicality."

You get most of your musical attention as a member and manager of the Town Criers (Weston's male a cappella group). It's well known that you guys can have a good time, but what is your favorite part?

"Joining the Criers was one of the best decisions I ever made. What was once a group of ten halfway committed guys that sometimes liked to sing on Sundays has grown into a brotherhood of highly dedicated musicians whose 2008 album has sold in six countries on iTunes. I could not be prouder about being the manager, and while we make what I can honestly say is real music, what separates the Criers from the rest of my ensembles is the chemistry. As someone who went to an all-boys camp for eight summers, I know what it's like to have friends that become brothers. The Criers fit the bill. We work hard, but we laugh and have a good time. We once had a successful gig in Boston, and to celebrate we all went out for dessert. Of course we couldn't leave without singing to the hostess, which landed us with a free crème brûlée. That's Criers in a nutshell."

Mr. Fuller seems to run his group in a style unique to the genre of soul and funk. What do you take away from the Funky bunch?

"I once said, 'Mr. Fuller, I can't sing today - I'm sick.' His response? 'Stevie Wonder never calls in sick. You're singing.' And with that, I was singing Wonder's *You and I* in two shows for one of our district's youngest elementary schools. Life in the Funky Bunch has a much different flavor. Rehearsals are lax. The schedule is lax. But there are two things that are consistent - serious talent and serious soul. The Funky Bunch is a group of about twenty students [from WHS]: full rhythm section, six piece brass section, and about eight vocalists. You see, nowadays there aren't a lot of places for a white boy to have soul. In FB I can feel it. During a show at school for Black History Month in 2008 we played EWF's September, and it remains one of the greatest performances I've ever played in. In a crowd of about 680 there must have been at least 350 people dancing. That's soul, baby . . . pure, homegrown soul.

If you had to sum up your music career in one paragraph, what would you say? In essence, what's the point?

"I'll tell you the point. The point is that up until my parents divorced, around the time I was twelve, I would hear my father every Sunday morning blasting one of those CDs. The point is that I loved music before I knew I loved it. Now there isn't a week where I don't have some major musical commitment and not a day where I don't hum or listen. What was once racket has become my soundtrack. Music is my constant. It comes in so many flavors and variations but it's all about life, liberty, and the pursuit of happiness . . . throughout middle school, high school, and college. Music is all of up and all of down and all of me."

-JC, Musician

*Mock interview with *Rolling Stone Magazine*

CURTAIN CALL

Since my days of striking out at tee-ball, I've clung to

the performing arts and refused to let them go. While

most boys my age get their adrenaline rushes from

football, hockey, and guerrilla warfare, I find mine

in applause.

From my debut as a very vocal Farmer MacGregor in a silent preschool rendition of Peter Rabbit to the Scarecrow in the Wizard of Oz, I love nothing more than taking to the stage and winning the hearts of millions. I get the most intense thrills producing mass laughter and making elderly men giggle in a way that, if their pals were around, would lose them the invite to the next fishing trip. When I set foot onstage, I automatically assume responsibility for the audience's amusement, and take it upon myself to keep everybody interested. I consider it the most rewarding challenge to home in on what tickles an audience; and I love nothing more than the instant gratification after taking such a risk and receiving thunderous response. Unlike the world of the cinema, the audience members of a play are their own camera, where they have the option of focusing on anything they wish. Therefore, there are times to shine and times to blend, which I have learned over the years.

Curtain call is what I love most about theater, because it is the immediate paycheck for one's individual success during a show. I cannot think of any other place where a group of people will howl for you for simply your standing on stage and bending over. Curtain call is like 600 hugs condensed into one giant sound that does not invade your personal space. Bowing is the most humanizing element of theater, for it frames the individual and rips away the mask of any character being played. Every time I bow, it feels like I'm saying, "That was me, what'd you think?" And the applause says, "We love you more than we love our families!" In a way, the theater establishes a sense of public intimacy, because such an intense focus of such a large group of people makes it become one entity. This makes me feel personally connected to the audience, making the experience truly wild. The bond among cast members is also something special; every show is like a war, with the veterans afterwards always having so much to share, and forever.

Exposing so much to a bunch of strangers is unearthly; but it's the essence of theater, and it builds a tacit respect between player and audience. Even if it means making one tiny girl's theatrical experience more fun, the performing arts are by far my juiciest reward.

THE INCOMPARABLE GOD OF FUN

When he approaches the dance floor, the crowd roars, teenage girls squeal, and chaperones are still not happy about throwing away their Friday night. He parts the sea of dancers better than Moses could ever do, and centers himself inside a bare circle on the linoleum floor. He stands with his weight shifted onto his left foot and his hand rested sensuously on his forehead, elbow tastefully bent. And then, without warning, he unleashes a storm of movement that has the intensity of a jungle cat and the fluidity of a mountain stream. His name is Jeremiah, and sometimes it's easy to forget that he has Down syndrome.

Late into my freshman year, I happened upon my school's Best Buddy program - an organization that pairs up mentally handicapped students with other students for one-on-one friendship.

Thinking I'd be giving a helping hand in the program, playing an occasional game of Uno with one of the guys, I was a little thrown on my first visit, when I heard someone in the corner calling "Hey Skinny" in my direction. When I turned to see my heckler, I noticed that he was dressed like James Dean - clad in a leather jacket, Harley Davidson hat, and raggedy jeans that had "menace" written all over them. Almost immediately his tough guy persona melted away with a few booming laughs; and, with a playful smack on my back, he introduced himself as Jeremiah. With wit, charming dishonesty, and dance moves to make the Boston Ballet yell "Uncle," he remains one of my closest companions.

I have always been drawn to people who like to laugh and make others laugh. Comedy runs thick in Jeremiah's veins. He writes his own material, pantomimes, and does an impression of Tim Allen that drives the ladies wild. His performing talents do not stop with comedy, however. At my first visit, he made sure I saw his skills of dance and he made sure he saw mine. We were impressed with each other, so we choreographed our own duet - never the same twice but always a hit on any Best Buddy dance floor we tore up. But, alas, it was known that he was a better solo act; and I felt wary of bringing him down, so I stepped off the scene. Later that season, I watched him single-handedly win the heart of every girl in the program. At the annual St. Patrick's Day tri-town dance, there is a bunch of groupies that nearly cry when they see the man do his Michael Jackson routine. Of anyone I have met - including foreign exchange students, a perennial hit - Jeremiah is the most enjoyable to have at a dance. He was either born without or at some point in time misplaced his self-conscious gene, making him an incomparable god of all that is fun.

Another hefty facet of his personality is his love of women. Any woman that he happens upon, whether a teenager, my sister, a 20-year-old with a massive boyfriend, a married woman, or an elderly librarian, Jeremiah has a heartfelt appreciation for their ownership of that second X chromosome. Many guys who have seen him in action are jealous; I know I am. I had always considered myself a skilled aspirant in the game of courtship, but I was devastated when I saw this Casanova in action. With a simple "Hello Ladies," he gets more hugs than a child in Disney World. Knowing Jeremiah has changed my perspective on people with Down syndrome. Jeremiah has taught me to push aside the fact that he has a disability; while it may hinder his ability to take a test or to write a paper, it has no effect on his spirit. Upon entering the program, I expected to be a good pal to the students and show them how to enjoy themselves. Little did I know that Jeremiah was not looking for a leader into good times - but instead someone to follow him into a world of merriment that he himself had already created.

Motivation Is a Dream in Work Clothes

It was September 15 of my sophomore year - the first game of the football season. I was notable as the undersized Nose Tackle, flanked on my right by a teammate who stood 6' 1" and 240 lbs, and on my left by another teammate who stood 5'10" and 190 lbs. Dead ahead was the opposing Center, who stood 6'0" and 195 lbs. And there I was, the lone sophomore on my team, surrounded by seniors and standing 5'8", 150 lbs. Need I say more? In the second quarter of the game, we were on our 40-yard line. The play was "Dive Left," right at me. The opposing Center, Guard, and Fullback all headed straight for me, with a combined weight of 570 lbs. There's no guesswork as to what happened next; it was a lesson in physics: I went to the ground like a dead man. This was my first varsity football game for The Rivers School and we were playing St. Mark's. That play was repeated time and again; it was a bloodbath, and I was the victim. Although it was uncomfortable and painful, I kept coming back play after play. That is the one thing I was proud of that day.

Flash forward. It is September 14 of my junior year; again the first game of the season, and again against St. Mark's. I was the same height, but 25 lbs. bigger; 3 tenths of a second faster in the 40 yard dash; and bench pressing 45 pounds more than the previous year. I was ready to prove myself a dominant player. I would not be trampled again. "Dive Left," they called their favorite play: Three opponents all coming at me. But this time I beat the center before the guard could lend a hand, and steamed right toward the fullback - down he went to the grass, like the dead man I was last year, except he went down 3 yards behind his own line of scrimmage. As someone said, "Motivation is a dream in work clothes"; it's the ideal I have followed on and off the field. I had spent a year working hard to achieve my dream of being an integral part of the team and a dominant player. Gaining 25 pounds in muscle between my sophomore and junior year was no easy task. The latter half of my sophomore year consisted of eating right, and a lot; two-hour grueling weight workouts; and sprinting seven quarter miles in succession. Although spring and summer workouts were tough, they were rewarding. My hard work won the respect of teammates and coaches. I learned to lead by example, and I exceeded my own expectations when my teammates voted me captain. I cherish and honor the opportunity for leadership. Football has become more than a game. My teammates are brothers and my coaches my mentors.

After the season ended I got to work. As captain I would not only have to set an example for younger players, but also for fellow seniors. Since junior year season ended, I have gained an additional 25 pounds, and dropped another 3 tenths of a second from my forty yard dash time. I am now 6 tenths faster than I was two years ago, and 50 lbs. bigger. With these gains, I have developed the confidence I need to be a dominant player, a team leader, and achieve the goals I set for myself.

"Motivation is a dream in work clothes." I have put this ideal into action in all aspects of my life, in the classroom and in other leadership and extracurricular activities. I plan to put the ideal into action as well in college and in my career and my life after

QUIET HEROES

Almost one hundred miles long through the tough crystalline rock of the Swiss Alps, the longest tunnel in the world is coming to life. Thousands of men and women risk their lives drilling and excavating the Gotthard Tunnel for a paycheck that doesn't match the dangers of the job. My family travels to Switzerland every other year to explore the small town of Sedrun where my grandparents live. We dual-citizens enjoy both the old-fashioned and new-age characteristics of Swiss culture in the Alps. As Sedrun is a station along the planned tunnel, I have been fascinated by the landscape of this project. The workers making this tunnel possible will never be remembered as Mahatma Ghandi, Martin Luther King, Jr., or other heroes on the world's stage, but as Henry David Thoreau once observed, "The hero is commonly the simplest and obscurest of men." The men and women of the tunnel will never be elected to a Hall of Fame, nor will any have a statue erected in his or her honor, but each must feel the satisfaction that comes with accomplishing something that makes a lasting impact on a place they love. Coming home, I thought about how heroism presents itself in everyday life in small, but very important ways.

This past school year was the last for our retiring principal, Charlie Ruopp, presenting a new challenge for our community. Along with nine other teacher-appointed students, I interviewed five candidates for the open principal's job. I thought about what Thoreau had written and sought a principal who would not try to do anything spectacular, but rather would quietly make a difference in our school. All the finalists were extremely well qualified, but I was looking for that "great communicator," one who listened well and spoke forcefully. I advocated for one candidate on that basis and he was appointed to the position. It was a challenging process, but afterwards I felt that even if I will never be remembered for helping to choose Wayland's new principal, I have the knowledge and satisfaction that I built something for our school and its future.

Quiet heroes may be obscure but make a difference in many ways, even in sports. All-Stars and MVPs attract the most attention and recognition, yet games and championships are won more often by the everyday heroes doing the little things that contribute to a team's success. In the spring of 2006 our varsity baseball team was in the sectional finals, with a small lead and two outs late in the game. With the bases loaded an opposing player hit a fly ball just over the infield, and noticing that my teammates were as still as stones, I sprinted, dove, and made the catch, preserving our lead. An inning later we won the game and the sectional championship. As a sophomore I was certainly not the most skilled or flashiest player on the team, but when hard work and effort are put into play every day, championship teams are created.

As with the hardworking men and women of the Gotthard Tunnel, I will probably never be handed a golden plaque nor have a statue created in my honor. Contributing to a team's success with the utmost effort eventually creates something great, whether it be a hundred-mile tunnel, a new school atmosphere, or a championship team. As Thoreau said, heroism and leadership most often come from ordinary people.

Don't Tap on the Glass, You Might Frighten the Animals

When I was seven years old, just when I had reached the point of clearly defined friendships at school (I even had a best friend!), my parents took my brother and me upstairs to their room, sat us down, and told us that within the next two months, we would move to South Africa. This wasn't such a tremendous surprise to me – Both my parents are South African, and I had spent a piece of every summer in my childhood with relatives in Johannesburg.

My real question was why. It was all a bit too complicated for me to understand at the time – something about the new responsibilities of my Dad's job required him to travel to South Africa to set up the new wing of the office. I didn't really get it then. To me, it was all just the next adventure, the next game. I broke the news to my friends about a week later. It was only after I told my friends that it really hit me – I was going thousands of miles from practically everyone and everything I knew for an undetermined length of time.

I was angry. I was one mad little seven-year-old. I tried to hide it; it was probably as hard for my parents or my brother as it was for me. I told all of my friends that we would be leaving a week earlier than we actually were. I didn't want any of the prolonged goodbyes, the final play-dates. That would have made it real, and the last thing I wanted was for my exodus to a strange land to be real.

Flash forward six months. I'm the foreign kid in a school of hundreds. Me, the American boy, with the accent I couldn't shake and the clothes that just weren't right and the movies that no one had heard of and the songs that no one liked. I was that kid, the outsider who ate lunch alone sitting on the stairs, the kid who biked for hours in his own driveway for lack of a better activity. I was the outsider looking in, and I became determined to belong.

Step one: Ditch the accent. Well, that wouldn't work, so instead, I took on South African mannerisms of speech. I used South African slang; I pronounced words differently (Aluminum, for instance, took me a week to get right). I became one of them. Step two: Get friends. I became less of a bookish recluse and more of the class clown. I would be the kid who purposely tripped just so everybody would laugh, and then, with a flourish, I'd bow. I became that kid, and in doing so, I joined forces with every class clown in the school. We were the kids who laughed the loudest during lunch, who played the weirdest games at recess, and more often than not we were the kids who were beaten up the most. I took my blows with pride. It meant that I was one of them, finally. I belonged.

The next two years were arguably the best in my childhood. I had friends, I had relatives (a luxury for me, being that they all lived in South Africa), I had what every eight to ten year old boy wanted. I had it made. Then came another one of those long night talks. It seemed that my father's work had finished in South Africa, and by the end of the year, we would have to go back to America.

Well, once more, I was angry. I didn't mind the going-back-to-America part. I did however mind that everything I had worked for was being once more taken away. There was nothing I could do and within the year, after some travel through Europe, we were back in America and I was once more on the outside looking in.

This time it was different. I didn't have to start at square one. I still had friends, although they were quite removed, and enough people knew me to stop me from going anonymous. But I was the South African American in a world of purebred Americans, and once more I was going to have to shift mannerisms, colloquialisms, and basically reconstruct who I was in order to fit in. On the plus side, however, my return coincided with my peers' shift from three elementary schools to one massive middle school. Everyone was a bit shaken up from the move, which left me with more leeway to decide who I was.

It took a while this time, due to the new idea of cliques. Everyone in school had suddenly decided to stop being everyone's universal friend and start spending time with just a small group of similar kids, and thus the clique was created. I made the choice to join the funny clique, which is where many of my former friends had wound up and my talents as the South African class clown came in handy. More often than not, during those first two years, my wacky ways landed me in trouble, and after a while, I became less of a class clown and more of a bright kid who cracks jokes sometimes. My experiences shaped who I became, and who I am today.

My three-year sojourn to South Africa changed who I was and who I am. It opened my eyes to the true size of the world. I had friends who hadn't traveled farther than outer New England while at the same time I was continent hopping. My travels also forced me to observe the people I am around. At the time, it was a necessity – study my surroundings, adapt to my surroundings, fit in to my surroundings. The analytical instinct still remains a big part of how I think. I study people; how they talk, how they act, how they carry themselves. It lets me understand people better, but it also keeps me partially separate from them. The scientist observing the apes can never turn himself into an ape. I was always behind a glass wall, watching, listening, understanding. I've always kept one foot out of my life. I can always take one step back from a situation, have a good laugh, and then step back in. I'm detached in a state of attachment.

If I could do it all over, would I move to South Africa again? Definitely. I have an outlook on life that most people don't get to have. I see things that most people ignore, and I understand things that most people pass by. My strange childhood of detached attachment made me the person I am today, and I wouldn't change that for anything.

LIFE'S CURVE BALLS

"It's not whether you fall down; it's whether you get back up." The line is from Vince Lombardi; it has become the sometimes mantra of my life or, variously, the bittersweet tag-line to the movie of my life - one that could not have been earned without, to my dismay, a variety of challenges and disappointments. In each case they have been challenges or disappointments proudly overcome.

I have heard the expression "into every life some rain must fall"; if that's true, my junior year was a torrential downpour. Within a little over a calendar year, I lost my three surviving grandparents: my father's mother and both of my mother's parents. This meant no more exchanging gifts with Nana at the Jewish holiday of Hanukkah and an end to her loving packages of my favorite cookies from my favorite Florida bakery; no more drives to Pennsylvania to spend Easter with the Catholic side of my family, greeting me with an endless supply of clams and shrimp. Although deeply upset, I realized that I could do one of two things: either dwell on losses, letting my mind be consumed with melancholy, or I could stay emotionally staunch - remembering and mourning my grandparents, but also continue on with my everyday life. I chose the latter. During the school year there were many books to be read and papers to write, and so, when we traveled to Florida or Pennsylvania for funerals, the work piled up. After returning home, I'd fight through emotions and work hard to catch up, as well as remain a stalwart role model for my younger sister, who looked to me for support. Perhaps I inherited resilience from my Nana, who was diagnosed with emphysema two years before she passed away. Despite frequent hospital stays, she always gathered up strength to spend time with us - whether at my sister's Bat Mitzvah or, when we visited Florida, going with us to the orange groves to pick fresh oranges.

Perseverance is a word with two denotations: the first mental fortitude, the second physical resolution. From the spring of sophomore year to the spring of junior year I have had ample opportunity to test my physical mettle, injured time and time again on the baseball diamond. In tenth grade, I was legging out a slow ground ball when the first basemen bent to scoop a low throw and I ran full speed into him, my hip crashing into his shoulder. Someone said they learned how a "Sharon High School Eagle really soars," as I flew through the air and hit the ground, separating my shoulder. Out for ten games, I worked with a PT who, fortunately, was also a past college baseball star; as I improved, he began throwing me batting practice. Because of the rigorous workout program he established, I was able to make my come-back appearance at the State Tournament playoff game and actually went on to play my best game of the season. But my return to the diamond was short-lived; in the fourth game of the American Legion summer season, I badly sprained my ankle and found myself back with the PT. This time we worked on leg strength and continued further conditioning of my shoulder. As a result, I emerged much stronger. "Every adversity is an opportunity," they say, and I was trying to make it so.

With my newfound strength, I began the year with a .440 batting average, near the top of the league. In the eighth game of the year, I was racing home to score the go-ahead run and began bending my knees to slide when I saw that the throw had gone wild and the ball was bouncing around the backstop - like a pinball. I decided not to slide, but too late. When I tried to continue to run, my knee hyper extended - two bones collided and fractured. Once again, I found myself in the all too familiar physical therapy office; the PT was now one of my best friends. The doctors had predicted that the healing process could take two months; but, with hard work, I conditioned muscles around my knee and returned to the field early, again stronger than prior to the injury. Now I persist in strengthening every area of my body, previously hurt and not. I am optimistic about the next season, hoping to raise my lifetime school batting average above its current .340.

My ability to persevere is not one I wish to exercise often; still, it is one of my proudest qualities. I am glad to know that, whenever life throws me a curveball, I will be able to greet it with moxie and a smirk - knowing that, when it crosses the plate, I will be able to knock it out of the park.

SLOW TO JUDGE OTHERS

"In my younger and more vulnerable years my father gave
me some advice that I've been turning over in my mind
ever since. 'Whenever you feel like criticizing any one,' he
told me, 'just remember that all the people in this world
haven't had the advantages that you've had.'"

--Nick Carraway
*from **The Great Gatsby***

*Since the beginning of my junior year in high school,
Nick Carraway from **The Great Gatsby** has influenced
how I am as a person. I deeply respect his character
and value the way he refrains from judging others until he knows them as they truly are. In life, many ado-
lescents and some adults tend to use a first impression
to judge one's entire character. I believe that it is better
not to form a judgment about someone than to make
a false or incorrect judgment. I avoid a quick judgment of a person's character before I learn sufficient*

information about that person, preferring instead to give others the benefit of the doubt. For instance, when driving, encounters with foolish acts committed by other drivers are frequent. To control road rage, I manage to find a good reason for the driver's error.

I try to emulate Nick's ability to observe and study human nature as he encounters various people. I try to learn what habits and forms of behavior are common in human nature so I can avoid criticizing people when they show human frailty. When I find something in a person's character that displeases me, I make a permanent effort to keep that flaw from ever becoming a part of my character. In conversations, it bugs me when someone responds to something I say before I am finished talking, which leaves us talking at the same time. Therefore, I listen carefully to what people say and if I speak when they are not finished talking, I immediately catch myself. Generally, I try to take the negatives in others and turn them into positives for me, a quality Nick uses as he assesses the unappealing qualities in the novel's various characters.

Nick was one of the few characters in The Great Gatsby who worked honestly and spoke truthfully. Like Nick, I choose to be true to myself and to work to improve and develop my character. Being true to oneself is very important. In my case, it prevents me from submitting to peer pressure, makes me an active participant in classes, and provides me with a steady degree of self-esteem. Nick was a very moral person because he was brought up that way and stayed true to his own moral feelings and virtues. Gatsby, Nick's friend and opposite, had no moral center, because he had abandoned and tried to forget his past, from which his morals originated. He no longer knew who he was because as Carson McCullers put it, "In order to know who you are, you have to have a place to come from."

Nick has influenced me in many ways. Thanks to him, I manage to reserve my judgments of others and learn from the things that tempted me to make judgments in the first place. Such values have increased my interest in philosophy, psychology, and anthropology, which I will most likely choose as majors in college. These traits have provided me with the trust of others, and continue to fuel my pride in myself.

A Prayer for Peace

Dateline Rome.
Venite Adoramus
Venite Adoramus
Venite Adoramus Dominum

As soon as I stepped inside the enormous stone structure 3,000 miles from my home, I took a deep breath of the incense which had saturated the air. As I felt the holy air enter my body, I was comforted knowing that I was present in the house of God for such a special occasion.

Sitting in a folding chair, shoulder to shoulder with an Australian family, and behind an African family, I was speechless. The beauty of the architectural phenomenon surrounding me, far surpassed anything I had ever seen before. Everything in the building was so ornate and expertly crafted, from the marbled Corinthian pillars which enclosed the sitting area, to the intricate domed ceiling above me. It was remarkable to see the history of Catholicism memorialized throughout this spectacular cathedral. Then as I turn to my left, I saw the most humble, yet most powerful symbolism of all. My eyes brought me to the scene depicting the foundation of

Catholicism- a nativity scene depicting the birth of Jesus.

Three months prior to my family's Christmas Eve visit to Saint Peter's in the Vatican, thousands of people lost their lives in the tragic events of 9-11-01. While my family and I were very apprehensive about traveling during such a period of world turmoil, we decided that the commercialization of Christmas was blinding us from the real meaning and purpose of such a widely celebrated holiday. Despite the threats of terrorism, my parents, my three younger sisters and I decided to travel to Rome in search of the religious meaning of the holiday and our true values in life.

Nearing the conclusion of midnight Mass celebrated by Pope John Paul, my eyes once again were fixated on the humble crèche. During the final moments of mass, the frail Pope placed a replica of baby Jesus into the crèche. During a time when the world was in turmoil, my core values in life became very clear.

As I felt the powerful 747 jet lift from the Italian soil, I held a simple medal in my hand and realized the power of its meaning. On the medal, created by Pope John Paul, were the symbols Alpha and Omega. In the center of the two symbols, there was a large P. This symbol represents the values of the Catholic Church, peace from the beginning to the end. Everyday when I look at this necklace, I am reminded of the amazing pilgrimage which helped me realize my core values- my love for my family and my dedication to goodness in the world.

A Life is Only Important in Its Impact on Others Lives

When the season started, we had no idea what to expect. Would the kids be outgoing? Would they behave? And, most important, would we have fun?

As young adult, I have enjoyed working with and making a strong impression on young children. In the winter of 2006, my friend Will and I coached a 12-year-old boys youth basketball team. We were hoping to build new friendships, have fun, and teach young men always to exhibit sportsmanship and strong character on the athletic field. As soon as Will and I thumbed through our roster, nervously shook each parent's hand, and had our team shoot around, we knew that we would be having an exciting and successful six weeks. Despite being very competitive, I knew it was important to befriend my players and to teach them morals that would stick with them all their lives.

At our first practice, Will and I began by asking each player his name and a random question about basketball, to break the ice. Right from the start we could tell that a few kids were friendly and outspoken, which foreshadowed the spunk and chemistry our team would possess all season. I made it clear that the main purpose of our season was to have fun, but that it would be a lot more fun if everyone put forth his best effort and all worked together on the court. From the first practice all were passing the ball to each other and hustling the entire time. I realized that my method of creating a fun yet hard-working environment had sent the right vibe. We won our first four games. Every week all ten would show up to practice energized and ready to work hard, so that they could not only improve but also challenge each other. This friendly competition that Will and I created proved to the kids that, if they worked hard for us, we would reward them with more playing time and more fun. Whether it was foul shots, sprints, or simply a scrimmage, we pushed the kids as hard as they could go. The persistence and courage apparent every Friday proved that each had a solid work ethic. All they needed was to be motivated by people whom they respected and could look up to.

Coming into the season, Will and I did not want players to dread coming to practices on Friday nights. From the minute we introduced ourselves to our twelve-year-olds, Will and I were constantly cracking jokes and making fun of each other. Everyone on our team was accepted - no matter if short, tall, skilled, or quiet. We made sure each and everyone was comfortable coming to practice. Along with all the kids being friends, I became close to the boys and would talk with them every week about sixth-grade gossip, girls, and if they had acted conceited (a no-no) toward players on other teams. I enjoyed proving that it did not matter that I was five years older; we still had a lot in common and we could carry on a conversation.

An example of chemistry and respect on our team was when Duncan, one of our less skilled players, was having trouble making foul shots. In a foul-shot drill, at the end of practice, for some reason he could not make a shot. After ten missed foul shots - and a lot of encouragement from his teammates - he finally sank a foul shot and felt a huge sense of relief, as his teammates congratulated him. In our game the next day, Duncan got fouled and was forced to shoot two foul shots; he swished both, smiling with pride as he ran back on defense.

In the six weeks I spent coaching ten boys previously unknown to me, I had developed a friendly bond with each and showed each what it meant to work really hard to attain individual and mutual goals. Our laid-back yet competitive aura allowed kids to have fun, which caused them to push themselves, not only to become better basketball players but better people.

Jackie Robinson had as his motto these words, which are engraved on his tombstone in Queens, NY: "A life is important only in the impact it has on other lives." I would like his motto to be my motto, something to work on every day.

ALL THINGS FLOW
FROM WATER

There is an Ottoman saying, which is found on many fountains built over the 400 years of Ottoman rule: "All things flow from water." And why wouldn't that be the case; after all, we live on the water planet, "the pale blue dot," as Carl Sagan called it. As a rower, I have a fantasy (as can occur in the delirium of a 2,000-meter hard row) that I meet in distant space a being from a far-off solar system, who says, "Oh yes, Earth, that's the Water Planet, isn't it? Do you row a lot there?" And the answer is Some of Us Do. I took to rowing, so to speak, like a fish to water.

Rowing has given us much more than shells gliding on water. I am a great fan of baseball, but I get tired of what's said of how baseball is the sport that's given us the best writing. It's not true. It's rowing. Here are a few choice examples. (I love math so I'm especially fond of this story.) The Oxford mathematician, Charles Dodgson, better known as Lewis Carroll, came up with his story of *Alice in Wonderland* while rowing with little Alice as his coxswain. He called out the story as he rowed, making it up as he went along, just to please little Alice and keep her at her post. Again, it's likely - a fantasy coming out of the delirium of rowing. Some have accused Carroll of being on drugs, but rowing IS a drug. I often say the hardest thing about rowing is NOT thinking about rowing. I don't know if Thomas Wolfe rowed on the beautiful rivers of his native North Carolina, but it sounds so, from his titles: *Of Time and the River, The Web and the Rock, The Far and the Near,* and *Look Homeward Angel* - a rower looking astern while rowing ahead. Rowing is a lot like life, in that regard, because one can never analyze the future; only analyze the past as it drifts off your stern. I think, too, of Harlem Renaissance writer Langston Hughes, whom we studied in school last year.

I've known rivers ancient as the world and older than human blood in human veins. My soul has grown deep like the rivers.

But the title that best describes my life on the water comes from a writer whom I'm guessing never rowed - it's Dickens's *The Tale of Two Cities.* While the cities he refers to are Paris and London, I think of one of the two cities in my tale as The Most Serene One. (In Italian it would be *La Serenissima,* the nickname for Venice, the city of water.)

In the grey light of early morning, at 5 AM each day, I enter that city. Not even the fish are awake. All is quiet, the water flat. But suddenly the serenity is shattered. A city is transformed. Shouts are heard; the eight-man rowing shell is shoved hard off the dock, sending ripples out into the water, breaking its glass surface. Orders are barked. Eight oars move in unison, propelling the boat into new waters never before touched. A philosopher said, "You never step in the same river twice." But you also never row in the same river twice. Each new stroke remains a venture into a part of the city never before touched. Sounds from the boat echo off "the city's walls," they carom off the shores. In this *Tale of Two Cities*, in moments, a city is transformed. Eight rowers create enough surge, work, noise, and echo to transform *La Serenissima*, The Most Serene One, into a modern burly city: The Turbulent City.

I don't know where rowing will take me - what "cities" lie ahead. But I know rowing will always be there, a part of everything else in my life. As the poet Anne Sexton wrote,

I am rowing, I am rowing
Though the oarlocks stick and are rusty.
But I am rowing, I am rowing . . .

Pointless Science
or Watching Nitrogen
Get Excited

It had seemed like a crazy idea at the time - and still

does - but I built a laser as an Honors Physics Project.

Film images of laser death rays' eating up the earth

in attempts to kill the Good Guy filled my mind and

poisoned early research, along with palpable fear of

severed retinas.

Still, I was able to produce a functioning nitrogen laser in the three-month time span allotted. I did so under the tutelage of my uncle and fellow science-lover Neal Van Wyck (a true-to-life scientist). Together, we collaborated for hours and drove many miles to each other's houses (he lives in Vermont, I in Massachusetts) to create this beast of a project. I also became a regular at the "You Do It" electronics store.

The premise of our laser is built on what are called "capacitors," which are charged with electrical current. The capacitors are partially open to air and partially isolated in a Plexiglas vacuum. Inside the vacuum, the two capacitors are separated by just 1 cm (four-tenths of an inch). When one capacitor is discharged - the current removed - the laser starts to function. The electrical discharge creates a "potential difference" in current and the potential difference doesn't make the capacitors happy. The other capacitor desperately seeks to equalize the current; and the only way for it to do so is by sending electrical current across the 1-cm gap to the other capacitor. So, electrons are shot across this gap, but, slyly, we placed miniscule "roadblocks" that the electrons must brush past on their journey. These roadblocks are actually nitrogen molecules in the form of nitrogen gas. (That was cheap; three-quarters of the air is nitrogen.) As electrons whiz by, they disrupt the otherwise content nitrogen, sending the nitrogen molecules briefly up into new energy levels. The molecules then fall back to their normal and lower energy levels; as they do, presto, they emit photons, or particles of light. A coherent package of such photons is called "a laser beam."

Somewhere, maybe along the dark Vermont roads, I realized my laser was an exercise in what others in America might call "pointless science." My laser could produce light. Period. It had no other function (other than the appreciated A on the project). No useful tool was created. No shocking discoveries were made. The exercise was full of frustration and a lot of play. Sometimes I felt like the nitrogen - things brushed past me, my excitement was raised and then lowered quickly, and occasionally, a beam of light went off in my head.

I did feel encouraged that the first laser came from an international race among scientists engaged in "pointless science." The winner was Howard Maiman from Malibu, CA. He created a ruby laser, but it was only a red light really. At the time, in 1960, it did nothing other than fuel the minds of science fiction writers. However, such "pointless science" did evolve and helped to improve our lives today. People can have 20/20 vision, listen to music recordings on CDs, or check out at cash registers with barcode scanners.

Lasers have made our lives so much easier. It is this "pointless science" to which I owe my father's life. He is here and with us because of it. When I was a small child my father suffered from a chronic cough for many months. After a doctor's visit on my mother's birthday, it was discovered that my dad had Hodgkin's disease, a dangerous but now curable form of cancer. For eons Hodgkin's killed people. However, with new medicines and new radiological techniques, based on scientific precepts once somebody's idea of "pointless science," he was able to make a full recovery. The real lesson I learned from my Physics project is the hope that we have the good sense to continue to fund basic scientific research. There's a lot of fun - and good science - in watching nitrogen get excited.

WHERE HAVE YOU GONE?

"Where have you gone, Joe DiMaggio? Our nation turns its lonely eyes to you." Simon and Garfunkel had the right idea, but perhaps we should ask, "Where have you gone, Jackie Robinson?" It has been too many years since the sports world has seen a man of such character and will. I met Mr. Robinson in history, and although he is no longer alive, his spirit and legacy live on. He was a warrior of sorts, yet not the type one might expect. While he did battle, he was not fighting with an army of thousands; in fact, he was fighting against an army of millions.

April 15th of 1947 seemed to be just an ordinary day. Mr. Robinson awoke to the sight of his sleeping wife and thought about the day's work. At Ebbets Field, the grass was as green as ever, the dirt as brown. The April sun mingled with the nippy Brooklyn breeze as nine men jogged through the grass and clay to their posts. However, that day was not just another day for it was filled with hatred and death threats. Yet, this was not just any professional baseball player. This man was Jackie Robinson.

Outside the entrance of Keystone Park on Coney Island there stands a bronze statue of Jackie Robinson and teammate Pee Wee Reese shaking hands. As soon as Jackie set foot in the clubhouse on that chilly April morning, Reese gallantly marched up to him, shook his hand and welcomed him to the team. Death threats had arrived from across the country and racial epithets were being hurled in many places. It is evident that Pee Wee admired Jackie's strength of mind, heart, and body in that he once said of him: "He had to... block out everything but this ball that is coming in at a hundred miles an hour. To do what he did has got to be the most tremendous thing I've ever seen in sports." Not only did Jackie Robinson integrate America's pastime, but he became a national leader off the field in the struggle for civil rights. He led both his team and the nation with dignity and integrity.

The athletic world is often a metaphor for society as a whole. Today's sports world is filled with "heroes" like Michael Vick, Bode Miller, and LaDanian Tomlinson, who once confidently stated, "If you're not cheating, you're not trying." There is now more than ever a need for an athlete to rise above it all, to achieve success with honesty and dignity, and to accomplish something in the greater community equal to his or her athletic ability.

It is a sad commentary on today's culture that I must travel sixty years in time to find a hero I can look up to as a baseball player and a leader in his society. To be able to meet such a man would be a dream come true. Although I may never be as revered as Jackie Robinson, I hope to make a difference in both the sporting world and in my own community. I look forward to the day that our nation can turn its lonely eyes to a new leader, someone who steps forward to guide us in new directions.

Essays from the hearts of girls

PINK PAJAMAS

Curious, I crept down the stairs as silently as possible in my pink pajamas. From the bottom of the staircase, I clutched my smiling clown doll and watched in fascination as I saw two bright blue words, against a background of black space, scroll across the screen: Star Trek. Images of unusual looking people appeared. I would later identify them as the crew of the Starship Enterprise.

Just as the action seemed to get underway, the music rose and a deep resonant voice spoke: "Space, the final frontier. These are the voyages of the starship Enterprise, to seek out new worlds, new civilizations...to boldly go where no one has gone before!" I watched a graceful little starship fly into deep space.

Off to my left, from the corner of my eye, I could see my father sitting on the couch. His arms were folded, his legs were stretched out, and his tie was loose at the nape of his neck. He gave the appearance of wanting to sleep, but he was still wide-awake. I was only six, and I never really had the chance to stay up late to watch anything. At that moment, my dad noticed that I was standing in

127

the doorway with my mouth open in amazement at what I was watching. He knew that I couldn't sleep, so he let me stay up with him to watch my first episode of Star Trek. I tucked myself in next to him. He said that I might actually learn something from Star Trek, regardless of bedtime. Of course, he would only let me stay up with him just this once. That hour spent with my dad was a special hour because it is the only time that I remember where my father was just my father, and not my employer or my teacher. There was none of that stiff awkwardness I usually feel around him.

You see, I have a hole in my soul, and it's in the shape of my father. Over the years, there has been an ever-present distance between us. I've heard great things about him: I've heard how great a doctor he is, how he was voted one of our city's "Top Docs." I've heard about what a kind and generous heart he has. I've heard about what a genius he is. I've heard about how I must take after him. To me, though, he was always more like a famous scientist that you idolize and can only love from afar.

My father has traveled a great arc in his life. A few years before the Cultural Revolution, my father's side of the family emigrated from Mainland China to Hong Kong, but they left him behind. My father had to live with his grandfather and his aunt. He went to a boarding school, but often he was homesick and went home, even though he was spanked for leaving the school. My father eventually joined the rest of his family in Hong Kong and then immigrated to the United States. My father had to work very hard in the American schools to earn good grades. Like his father and grandfather before him, he became a doctor and a father.

More than anything, I have wanted my father to say how proud he is of me. I wanted him to say that I did a good job without any kind of criticism at the end. So I have worked to make him proud. Aside from schoolwork, I rarely saw him or talked to him. Everything we did together, from flute lessons to boating, it was teacher and student, never father and daughter. I wanted to be able to talk to my father about anything but schoolwork. I can't. There is always this stiff awkwardness I feel around him. It always feels like teacher and student. Strict as he is, my father is my father, and he only wants to take care of me. I can't deny that.

Since the time when I walked down the staircase in my pink pajamas with my smiling doll, there is one loving connection that we have shared as father and daughter. That has been our life shared around Star Trek. The stiff awkwardness fades away, and things are looser. Laughter happens and friendly debates rage. My father bought most of the 268 Star Trek books I have as gifts. Somewhere in my mind, I know that those books were given to me out of love, even as I know that they were also meant to nurture my love of reading through something that the two of us shared.

In addition to books, he has added other fond objects to my collection of Star Trek memorabilia. One of my favorite gifts of all is a phaser. A phaser is a multi-tasking tool in Star Trek: it heats things up, it detaches things, and it's even a weapon for protection. My dad gave me the phaser for Christmas because he felt that it showed who I was - someone who multi-tasked, sometimes with mixed results. It's become an inside joke between us that, as when the phaser has too much pressure on it, it explodes; the same goes with my personality. According to my dad, it can be highly entertaining when that happens. All of it is said with a loving smile. He gave me the phaser four years ago; it still sits on my desk. It's my protector. As I write my essay, I look at it and smile, because I remember why it's there.

My mind returns often to the late night in my pink pajamas. I cherish the memory of that night, and what it means for me and for my dad.

THE TASTE OF VICTORY

I began to realize the great joy and power of running after joining the cross-country team my sophomore year. I have never been considered a good runner. Perhaps this is the reason why I made it my goal to join the team. Each time I set out to run a long distance, I would establish, accept, and pursue a challenge I had set for myself. As I continued, I began to find and exercise an internal strength I had only been dimly aware of before.

My runs of solitude had the sweet taste of satisfaction. At first my discomfort dissuaded any other thoughts, and a "get it over with" mentality made my first runs far from enjoyable. But repetition taught me to love pushing past the pain and to find an internal drive I had never known. My runs became a time where I consciously tested my limits. I learned to love the self-gratification that came out of my pursuit, and the dedication I learned from running had the unanticipated benefit of extending to and enriching other aspects of my life; it was not too long before I brought home the best report card I had ever achieved. The work I put into running qualified me for the cross-country team I had aspired to join, and my individual strength came to serve as a gateway to the benefits I would have never known had I continued to run in solitude.

I soon found myself running double the speed and distance. Running with three of the state's fastest girls was inspirational. Although they would be light years ahead in all the races, like me, these girls relied on the team and its energy to motivate them through practice each day after school. So, when these few girls led our team to the state championship, I knew that I had truly contributed; that along with the rest of the team, I had helped bring our team to the top. It was impossible to differentiate the top three runners from the rest of the team when we learned we had won the Division II State Championship. Even though cross-country is not considered a "team sport" per se, I learned that the possibilities of a group far exceed those of an individual. I came to realize that victory can be far greater, and far more satisfying, when shared with twelve other girls just as sweaty, and just as out of breath as me.

Building Educated Leaders for Life

"BELL exists to dramatically increase the academic achievements, self-esteem and life opportunities of children living in low-income, urban communities . . . We pursue our mission because we believe in the tremendous potential within all children – who we call 'scholars.'"
—*Bell Foundation Mission Statement*

Learning to read is difficult enough for most first graders, and it seems to be even more difficult for fifth graders who are surrounded by peers already reading chapter books. I had chosen to spend my summer working for the Bell Foundation, a nationally recognized after school and summer school program. Sitting with David and Shanaya outside in the hall reading a simple rhyming book with more pictures on one page than words in the whole book was clearly the last place either of these 'scholars' wanted to be. I was volunteer-

ing at the Mattahunt Elementary School to give special

attention to those fifth graders who needed extra help

in reading. While David and Shanaya couldn't read

from A Mouse's Wedding, *they still showed cleverness*

in recognizing the first letter of a word and shouting

out the first word they could think of that began with

that letter. I sat between them on a chipped wooden

bench pressed tightly against a yellow wall as the book

rested on my lap. On the wall to the right of me was

a mural of children of different races holding hands

and playing. I was hoping that the children who now

sat on either side of me could be this happy rather

than aggravated by being asked to spend their sum-

mer learning to read.

Word after word, David would jump ahead without taking the
time to sound out the letters before him, something he was very
capable of doing. At the end of what seemed like a painful ten
minutes of reading the story, I placed the list of missed words on
my lap. Trying to think about what could possibly make two fifth
graders who were delayed in their reading skills motivated enough
to take time to sound out simple words was a challenge. Then I

had it: a race with points leading up to a prize! It did not matter to them that I was completely unaware of what the prize would be for the student who received more points, as long as the word "prize" was involved. I tallied points as David pushed ahead of Shanaya, carefully sounding out words such as "moon" and "table."

The number of words on the list slowly diminished, and the tone of both students' voices perked up as the game became more intense and more points were given away. After David beat Shanaya in this "game," finishing with three more tally marks, his pride overtook the fact that the grand prize was nothing better than a warm hug from me. I led both students back into their classroom to join their peers in pushing in their chairs before they would line up for lunch. As I handed over the book and list of missed words to Ms. Rose, their teacher, her warm and appreciative "Thank you!" was cut off when David interrupted with an enthusiastic and repeated tap on her shoulder. "I didn't know reading could be fun!" he boasted.

THE PUMPKIN FESTIVAL

"The question is not whether we will be extremists but
what kind of extremists we will be. Will we be extremists
for hate or will we be extremists for love?"
--Dr. Martin Luther King, Jr.

What we are taught dictates who we become. My parents have instilled in me the obligation to bring help to others in need. Throughout my life, I have witnessed my family's unceasing generosity. Whether it was my mother's guiding my aunt legally and spiritually through her divorce, my father leading a fundraising drive for recreation centers, or my grandparents' giving up their seats in temple for an older couple, my family has taught me how to help others. One event in high school has galvanized for me the importance of giving back to the community.

For several years, a wonderful local company called Life is Good, Inc. has sponsored a "Pumpkin Festival" on the Boston Common to raise money for Camp Sunshine, a summer camp in Maine for children suffering from life-threatening illnesses and their families. The camp's goal is to give families a respite from doctors' appointments and hospital visits. The event had been successful in Boston, and so, in the fall of my junior year, I began planning an event in Weston that would be part of the larger Boston Pumpkin Festival.

The Boston festival was to take place on October 21st, which gave us just six weeks to plan our Weston event. I began to have regular conversations with the Director of Communications at Life is Good, Jim Laughlin, who had three goals. The first was to raise $500,000 for Camp Sunshine. While our Weston event would be free, we would ask those attending for donations to Camp Sunshine. The second goal was to set up a day of fun autumn activities for children of all ages. Jim constantly reminded me to keep it simple, stressing his "pumpkin-hot cocoa" theory, which states that a day of hot chocolate and pumpkin carving would provide plenty of entertainment for our first-time event. While I respected his caution, I was convinced our community could do more, and so I added music, kids' activities, and food sales to our agenda. The third goal was to carve enough pumpkins on October 21st to break the world record of 30,128 jack-o-lanterns carved in a single day. We would carve as many pumpkins as possible in Weston and transport them to Boston that night.

As chair, I was to recruit and organize a group of high school students to help achieve these objectives. A high school had never before participated in this Boston Pumpkin Festival so we needed a dedicated committee to plan the event from scratch. Thirty students representing every grade level and social group joined, and the enthusiasm was infectious. Kids would show up to meetings with wet heads from swim practice, with instruments tucked under their arms, or with friends in tow who wanted to help. We were creating a new Weston tradition. We all took our principal's favorite quote by Dr. Martin Luther King Jr. to heart because we had been given the chance to share with the community our love for service.

As October 21st approached, all details fell into place. I had become the face of the event and could barely move between classes without a student giving me a "pumpkin update." Fliers had been passed out to every elementary school student, raffle prizes donated, permits obtained, and our pumpkin carving tools had safely arrived.

On the day of the event, the sun shown brightly on a perfect New England autumn day. Student and parent volunteers worked the registration table, bake sale, pumpkin carving stations, and our kids' activities tables (including face painting, balloons, magic tricks, and pumpkin decorating). The school band struck up jazz tunes and children ran around in Halloween costumes. There is something magical about pumpkins. No one can resist the traditions that they represent, and no one can resist smiling when dipping a hand into an orange bowl of gooey seeds. One Life is Good company motto is, "We shall never know all the good a simple smile can do," and the hundreds of smiles I saw that day reminded me how important it is to share something you enjoy with friends and community.

By 5 o'clock that afternoon, we had carved 531 pumpkins and piled them onto a 24-foot U-Haul truck to be driven into Boston. With my friend's father driving a truck for the first time, and my friend and I sitting in the front seat next to him, it took us only 15 minutes to get to Boston and another hour to drive the next three blocks to Boston Common. Jim called me repeatedly while we were still in the truck to say that they still had not broken the record and would need our pumpkins by 7 o'clock, or it would be too late. When we made it onto the Common, volunteers lined the road shouting, "It's the Weston truck!" With the help of a dozen Boston volunteers, we frantically unloaded, numbered, and put a candle in every pumpkin, so that each could become part of the record. Twenty minutes later, Jim, normally a serious and reserved man, came running toward me with an enormous smile and his arms out for a hug, shouting, "You put us over the top, we broke the record!" As we were escorted around the Common that night, we were known by the Life Is Good staff as the "Weston kids who put us over the top."

In the end, 1000 people attended our festival and we raised over $12,000 for Camp Sunshine. With our donation, and many others from that day, Camp Sunshine built a new cafeteria and activities wing to make these families' summer experiences even more enjoyable.

I learned much that day. I learned that improving the quality of life for people who struggle every day is about sharing a common goal of support and healing. My actions confirmed my parents' belief that, as a member of the community, I have the ability and responsibility to bring happiness to the lives of others and that I ought to be an "extremist for love."

STRETCHING MY LIMBS

When I climb a tree, I start at the bottom. In cut off jean-shorts and a tucked in shirt: I feel the wet grass on the bottom of my bare feet. Then the moss comes, green and soggy with the occasional prickly spores. As I lift my right leg up (almost always the right and not the left), I feel the lower pieces of bark, those first pieces are the roughest and toughest of the whole tree. But once the toughest bark is surpassed, it becomes easier. The bark turns smoother, and the tree presents more notches for feet and hands. Then, comes the first branch; like a helping hand, the branch slopes slightly downward so one can grab on and then pull up to the next one. The first branch is thick, they get smaller and smaller as the tree grows taller. Also, as the tree grows taller, the branches are more closely spaced, making it easier, requiring less of a stretch from all four limbs (and neck).

Further and further up the tree I go, the ascent is thrilling. I can smell it, the bottom of the tree discharges a scent of age; often the subtle stench of rotting or drying leaves that have fallen off their branches only to become increasingly familiar with the dirt surrounding the tree, eventually melding with it. As I gain altitude, the smells change ever so slightly. The tree exudes a sense of freshness, the thinner branches contain a feeling of immaturity. I can often tell that some branches are unsafe to grab hold of. I know from experience that my weight would easily crack the weak limb, exposing the green guts of the young extension.

Climbing the tree is not merely a thrill, I gain a multitude of things when I climb a tree. The activity is not always that of a spontaneous nature, but can also be that of a therapeutic sort. I can breathe, think, daydream, the clock is not counting down to a specific deadline nor is it ticking to remind me that there indeed does exist a calculated time and place for every miniscule thing. Purely existing with birds and bees, to think or not to think, the rustling of squirrels scurrying up and down the trunk is a vacation that can be created in any place or at any time.

Once I find a place I feel meets my needs (at the top of the tree or just on a comfortable landing of sorts) I stop. Sometimes I sit and straddle the branch. Swinging both my legs back and forth, listening to songs stuck in my head: my in-brain iTunes contains everything from Aretha Franklin to The Red Hot Chili Peppers to Talking Heads, and even songs from the latest *Saturday Night Live* skit. In other cases, if the mood suits, I find myself sitting with my back flush against the trunk of the tree, my legs quasi-stretched out along a substantial sized branch. At these times, I find my mind truly drifts off into a world of its own. I dispel all stresses and think of lighter subjects. What shall I make for dinner, chicken with capers and lemon, or cheese ravioli with spinach and a light cream sauce? I remember wondering about my summer trip to Alaska: would I live the fantasy of Alexander Supertramp, or be destined to fare the same as mere mortal Chris McCandless as in *Into The Wild* by Jon Krakauer?

Finally, when I deem my pondering sufficient, or have taken in enough of the views (whatever they may be), I begin my descent. I turn to face the tree, looking down before every step to gauge my footing before resting all my weight. My trip down is slower than that of going up. I proceed with caution, knowing that there lies more risk in coming down; I press my body up close to the tree. Occasionally this results in small scratches on my cheeks, or bark scraps in my hair. As soon as my height off the ground is one of reasonable proportions, when I know a jump will not result in the breaking of both my ankles, I breathe. One quick deep breath is followed by a literal leap of faith. "Thwack": The thud of my feet hitting the ground mixed with the usual crack of a knee, I have landed back in the realm of reality.

But I'm not done yet. Just as I enjoy climbing the tree, I revel in taking in what the bottom has to offer. I walk towards a canvas tote bag I have left somewhere not far off from the base of the trunk and reach inside. Pulling out a paperback, the cover may read *A Snow In August* or *The Secret Life of The Bees,* maybe even the latest Harry Potter. But along with my book or schoolwork that I pull out to muse over at the bottom, I always have a green apple. "An apple a day keeps the doctor away" but a green apple at least once a day also happens to keep a smile on my face. I mosey back on towards the tree, plopping myself down and squiggling myself around until my back is nestled perfectly in with the tough bark. I take a first crunchy bite of my apple, it resonates deep within me; I can hear it, feel it in my ears and in my jaw. Being at one with the bottom of the tree is almost as rewarding as relaxing at the top.

It may be when I am done with my apple, or it could be hours, I sit, back to bark, taking in all the tree has to offer. I then put my arms on either side of me; with one strong push I am able to instantaneously pop up. I walk away, arms swinging, pep in my step. My day journey is complete. All I have as evidence are the lovely wet spots that have found a home on the back of my pants.

A Thousand Points of Light

Lining the ceiling of the Westborough Senior Center were purple streamers and paper hearts; they dangled over tables draped with red-and-white tablecloths, littered with Hershey kisses. The center's all-too functional cafeteria now looked like a disco - run by Cupid. As co-president of Interact, a community service organization, I looked around with pride that my fellow members and I had accomplished this transformation in a single afternoon. When the DJ arrived and began to play "My Funny Valentine," the anxiety that had plagued me for months, as we'd planned this event for seniors, began to ebb; I sat back and enjoyed Sinatra at his best.

I sent a group of members over to a huge basket, overflowing with tissue-paper roses - the ones we'd stayed after school to make a week earlier. The girls lined each side of the set of double-doors, and waited for fifty senior citizens to arrive. As each entered, he or she was given a tissue-paper rose. Although well aware the roses were fake, once they grasped the pipe-cleaner stem, many held the paper petals to their noses and graciously said, "These are lovely." Some couples arrived, hand-in-hand, wearing matching red sweaters, and headed straight for the dance floor. As they waltzed or jitter-bugged to a succession of songs, we all stared at them in awe - quite intimidated that we were no match for their classy dance moves. As the dance came to a close, we sat, scattered among the tables, engaged in conversation. Looking back, I realize that I enjoyed the company of the seniors as much as they seemed to enjoy ours. As the seniors departed - taking with them handfuls of chocolates and bushels of tissue-paper roses - I took away with me the warm feeling I felt in the room that day: the mutual respect and kindness exchanged between a group of high school students and a group of senior citizens.

THE ECONOMICS OF POVERTY

As the smell of pizza slowly wafted up to my nostrils, I fidgeted in my seat yearning for just one slice of the greasy cheesy concoction. Soon my attention shifted away from the food - just one room away - and I realized that the Southern behemoth to my right was still lecturing about the plague of poverty that wreaked havoc upon the local counties of Rowan, Bath, Elliot and Morgan.

So far, this experience had dismally disappointed my expectations. Months before, my youth minister had come to me with plans for a journey that might change my life. Three other teens and I had planned for weeks so that this service trip for a dozen youths would go off without a hitch. We were to fly down to Morehead, Kentucky, and work with a program called Frontier Housing. This program, with financial backing from the U.S. government, helps build low-income housing in many of the poorest counties in the state. Prior to the trip, we had learned of the poverty that spanned much of southern Appalachia and how it related to the area in which we would be working.

As I hailed from a quaint New England town, I was quite unsure of what to expect of this small Southern borough. Although I tried to keep an open mind, I kept drifting back to preconceived notions that had been created by television shows such as the Beverly Hillbillies. I tried to imagine the people to be similar to me and my comrades, but I could not quell the images of overweight old men with Southern drawls, chewing tobacco while waving their Confederate flags. Of course this image was only solidified when I met the head of the organization, Jim Ward. As he greeted me, he extended his massive hand just before shooting a muddy stream of tobacco into a cardboard coffee cup. "Welcome to Morehead. How are you today little lady?" he questioned in a deep voice. I tried not to recoil from his immense grip, and instead addressed him with a weak smile.

Of course, all of the introductions had ended hours ago, after we had first arrived at Morehead State University (where we would be housed). Now the group had been sitting and listening to Jim rattle off hundreds of facts and figures for two hours while at the same time, our pizza was getting cold in the other room. We were all exceedingly hungry, seeing that we had just endured two plane rides and one very long and uncomfortable bus ride, all without victuals. The only thing that was able to mollify the vociferous rumblings in my stomach was the distraction of watching the Kentucky scenery fly by my window. The crowded roadways and concrete overpasses near the airport sharply contrasted with the rolling hills covering the countryside. I had expected Morehead to be a bustling metropolis (since it housed a state university), yet it turned out to be quite the opposite. The main road was laced with a bank, a restaurant, a one-theater movie theater, and a few small shops. In fact, everything was so empty that I expected tumbleweed to roll through.

At this point, Jim rose out of his seat and I snapped out of my reflective state and back to attention. He was not yet finished with his recitation; instead, he was passing out sheets detailing the families for which we would be building houses. I was not trying to be insensitive, but it was difficult for all of us to pay attention after such a long day. Despite my fatigue and hunger, my ears perked up when Jim spewed out a certain fact. He explained that the yearly income for a certain family of five was $6000 a year. At first, I didn't think much about this figure until I began to do some quick math in my head. Six thousand dollars, divided by twelve months, was only $500 a month for the entire family. That averaged out to $100 a person a month, or $25 a week per person. That was about how much I spent on gas and lunch money; how could this family possibly survive? I had expected that theses families would not have a second home on the beach, but I never could have predicted how tight their financial circumstances would be.

I now felt guilty for ignoring the beginning of Jim's speech, and was determined to make up for it by listening intently to every word that crossed his lips. I felt as if I was being disrespectful to the families by not lending an ear to their predicament. Jim soon began to describe the mission of his group, Frontier Housing. Although the group relied on volunteer work, they also had more than a dozen full-time staff that worked hard to continue the operations. Those families who applied for houses through this program were also forced to work hard. According to government standards, they were forced to work innumerable hours on the completion of their house. This does not seem extremely difficult until one ponders the fact that the heads of these families probably worked long hours at numerous jobs. But, Jim continued to explain, our volunteer hours would help to diminish the amount the homeowners must complete.

Upon hearing this information, I was dying to put my idle hands to work doing anything. However, Jim's presentation was still not complete. He began to give us a very important economic lesson that proved to apply to many of the impoverished people in the area. He explained that many families buy trailers as a cheap housing alternative to a house. Yet, in the long run, this practice is more harmful than helpful. A trailer is considered a vehicle, such as a car, and therefore depreciates in value over time. Therefore, when a family invests in a trailer, they are actually hurting themselves, and it is a poor investment. In contrast, those families that are able to purchase a home are helping themselves. A house continues to appreciate in value, and therefore is a good investment. Unfortunately, the majority of people live in trailers and therefore are only continuing the cycle of poverty. On this note, Jim wrapped up his presentation noting that we should get some sleep, as the next day would be filled with hard work.

Despite that just an hour earlier I would have sprinted to grab a slice of pizza, I now shuffled slowly over to the greasy cardboard box, suddenly without an appetite. Instead of hunger, I was overcome with a sense of guilt, not only for ignoring Jim and his speech, but also for living so comfortably all my life while people had been suffering throughout the country. I was always aware that poverty flourished in Third World countries, but I had somehow been unaware of the suffering that existed right here in the United States. Although it was summer vacation, I had learned a very important lesson in economics.

My Future Mission:
Helping Children and Families

Some Self-Imaginings . . .

LAWYER - As I step into my office bright and early on a cool fall morning, my secretary hands me a manila folder to help me prepare for my case this afternoon. I sit down in my leather chair and open the folder to find many of my own notes on Mr. and Mrs. Jones's divorce case, along with various bills, documents, and other legal papers. I knew this case was going to be tough from the start, but I wanted to do everything I could to help Mrs. Jones gain legal possession of Emma, her seven year-old daughter. Mr. Jones not only cut off the money supply that once supported his family: he also took the house, leaving his wife and daughter to find an affordable apartment with what little money they had saved. The very last thing I want is to let that man gain full custody of Emma, letting him have everything he has ever wanted, and leaving his wife with nothing . . . PSYCHIATRIST - As I sip my caramel macchiato in hopes of warming myself from the numbing winter air of Chicago, I flip through my agenda to look at my appointments for the day. I glance down to see Bill at 9:00 a.m., Sarah at 10:30 a.m., and my favorite patient of all, Jordan, at 12:00 p.m. Having already listened to a two-hour seminar on the ideas of the child theorist Anna Freud, I am exhausted, but knowing that I get to see Jordan will help me make it through the day. Bright, funny, and witty are all words that describe Jordan's amazing personality, but you can't truly understand how great a kid he is until you meet him yourself. Each time I see Jordan, however, his little eight year-old face becomes dimmer and dimmer, as if his rough family situation is draining the life out of him. He just arrived home from Boston a couple of days ago, where he had been visiting his mother in the hospital for the past two weeks. Coping with the slow but sure death of a parent is rough enough for an adult, but the effects on an eight year-old boy are irreversible. I am trying to predict what my meeting with him today will be like, but for the life of me I can't even begin to guess whether Jordan will be shining brighter than ever, happy to have spent time with his mother, or whether he'll be completely burnt out, devastated by the reality check that has just slapped him in the face . . . **MAGAZINE EDITOR** - As I stroll down Broadway with the hot sun beating full-strength on my face, I wave my arm out past the edge of the sidewalk in hopes of catching a cab to One City Center, where I am interviewing Hillary Clinton about her stance on the No Child Left Behind Act. Although I am trembling a little, I am very excited to be doing my first high-profile interview on a topic that actually interests me, instead of the usual proofreading of my coworkers' writings so I can learn the ropes of conducting a proper interview. "I can do this," I think to myself, "and Vogue will absolutely love it." Once I catch a cab, I frantically review my papers and practice the questions as quietly as possible. "Mrs. Clinton, do you think that high stakes testing is improving the quality of education in America?" I speak slowly and calmly and try my best not to stumble over the words. "Will teachers teach to the test rather than giving a fuller education to the student? Does the Act have different consequences for children and families of different socio-economic backgrounds?" . . . **COUNTER TERRORISM AGENT** - Sitting at this desk all day is making me crazy, but as much as I want to go outside to take a deep breath of the sweet spring air, I refuse to do anything else until I can crack this case. I have been so close to solving it for the past few hours, but for some reason I can't seem to track down exactly where the President's daughter is located. A tracking device had been planted on her every morning before she left her house specifically for situations like this, but I just can't pinpoint exactly where she is. Frustrated as to why the tracker only shows she's been kidnapped and held somewhere in the giant state of Texas, I look away from the screen to give my eyes a five-second break. I do want to crack the case, but my main concern is that this ten year-old girl is being held hostage, and as of now there is nothing I can do about it. If she were my daughter, I would be completely distraught, so I can only imagine what kind of stress and concern the President and his wife are feeling at this time.

Whether I become a divorce lawyer, child psychiatrist, political editor for a magazine, Counter Terrorism Agent, or pursue any other job that I find fascinating in my future years, I know that all of the careers that I am interested in concern children and families in one way or another. The power of imagination has allowed me to envision myself working at various jobs that can fulfill my main interest, and promises the discovery of many more possible future paths. With Samuel Taylor Coleridge and the Romantic Poets, I believe that the imagination is "essentially vital" to a satisfying and productive life. My mind is ever-changing, and my interests are scattered over a wide range of specialty jobs, but my main concern is to help and benefit families and children in whatever way I can.

"My eyes make pictures when they're shut."
Samuel Taylor Coleridge

THE FARM SCHOOL

My mind is wandering from the cool breeze, to the soft sounds of birds, to the distant sound of the hose running in the garden, when all of a sudden my attention is brought to the sharp surprise of a rough wetness pushing against my foot. I look up to see Karissa, a Jersey cow, nibbling grass that I had been twisting between my toes. Lying in the cow pasture with Dandelion, another heifer, as a backrest is an exercise as routine in my summers as the beach is to so many of my friends. Here at the Farm School, a small dairy farm in western Massachusetts dedicated to teaching teenagers about their rural heritage, I reserve two weeks of my summer for the last five years as a welcomed escape from day to day life.

When I am asked as many times as there are grains of sand in the Sahara Desert why I actually pay this place to have me do manual labor, I always answer with a consolatory smile on my face. When someone with a zigzagged expression on their face asks me this age old question, I know that they will truly never understand the benefits of the relaxing, physically exhausting, comforting, and never tiring life on a dairy farm. The Farm School is the only place where I am reassured that every night I will have the same perfect feeling. It is one of utter exhaustion, but at the same time that is what makes it so great. I know every time the sun sets in Athol that I have given my all to help the animals, people and land at a place that has given me so much. I would never let anyone take from me a day that feels so organic, so right, and so much like life is supposed to be.

Looking out of my window from my bunk, I, yawning, am conquered by a sense of supreme accomplishment. When I see what I have brought about that day, all those little tasks that keep this place running, I can tell that the last sixteen hours had not been wasted. Every second of my days at the Farm School, from getting up with the roosters to feed the cows, goats and chickens, to working in the hot noon-day sun on fixing the chicken coop and tending to the garden, I cannot imagine living without. Sure, I could have been working on summer reading, taking out the trash or anything else that might need to get done at my house in suburbia, but the feeling that this is what people have been doing for thousands of years makes it feel so right. As I look upon a horse securely tied to a newly made and sturdy hitching post, sure I know that I have kept that horse just a bit safer, and that it is that much more convenient putting that horse's equipment on, but what I more see is my work put into that construction, as well as what others have put into bits and pieces of the rest of the farm. Many times in my life I have worked for hours on school projects that ten years later have nothing tangible to show for my labor. Yet I know that the bunkhouse, built by the groups of kids who first came to the Farm School, is still proving how important their work is.

Everyone who has ever asked me that question I have known to also say that who would want to live on a farm when we are in the age of computers, television and supermarkets; yet to me, those things have never given me a sense of accomplishment and right in the world. A pride in getting an A on a paper has never come close to the pride of finishing a project outside with a group of your closest friends who you just happened to have met three days ago. When you finish something as unique in this modern world as a fence or a hitching post, you connect with the others who worked on it because it is something so distinct and of its own kind. So yes, I may have to put a little more sweat into my summer camp than most, but I know that so much more is coming out of it.

My Tuesday Night Date

Matty in the morning! Kiss 108 FM! To most Bostonians the ring of this catchy tune is something you hear when waking up on a weekday morning or while driving to work. Although I, too, reluctantly drag myself out of bed for school to the sound of this familiar jingle, it has a different meaning for me. Matty in the Morning, radio personality on Boston's Number One Hit Radio Station, is my father.

My parents have been divorced since I was born, so Tuesday nights have always been dinner nights with my dad. For about two months, we will generally go to the same restaurant until we become bored with it and move to something else. This month we are really into Thai. I always look forward to Tuesday nights, because when my dad and I go out, it is like we are the only two people in the room. Some people might think that having a celebrity for a parent might prohibit a close relationship, just as having divorced parents would. Yet even with these two factors, our weekly dinners represent the wonderful intimacy of our relationship. When we are together, we love to people-watch, a prime source of raw material for our inspiration to perform. We have to work hard to avoid the mayhem that follows us wherever we go, seeing as we seek it out in order to create more amusement for our dinners. It seems that the weirdest fans approach my dad only on Tuesday nights. Waiters are constantly forgetting our orders and we are always seated next to couples with extremely odd quirks. Yet no matter the inevitable chaos, our goofiness makes it all part of the fun. After we finish with the weekly "boy talk," we move on to more important topics of discussion, like organizing my responsibilities for hair and make-up at my theater company, and whatever global issues draw our attention that day. My dad is also my favorite person to talk with about my future.

My dream is to become a professional actress. Because my dad is already in show business, I look up to him as a mentor and as tangible evidence that my dreams can come true. My dad did not discover his dream as early as I have found mine. Although originally he had studied to become an English teacher, he always knew that he had a particular skill with words and a talent for being in front of an audience. It wasn't until a professor asked him why he wasn't schooling to be an entertainer that he even considered becoming a disc jockey. After receiving this encouragement, he never looked back.

My dad has always been honest with me. He constantly reminds me that I have chosen the hardest profession in the world. While I want to perform on a stage in front of people and he prefers the audio effect of radio, we both appreciate the excitement that comes with entertaining any type of audience, whether they are in an auditorium or at home in their kitchen. "Never give up," he always tells me, and although this is a very clichéd saying, I feel that it has a special meaning coming from my dad. My dad started off as a DJ at a radio station that no one had ever heard of, and at an hour that no one was ever awake, and I am confident that I too may begin with a challenging job like this that will ultimately lead me to success. I know that I have the same passion for creating entertainment that he does, and that no matter the obstacles, I too will succeed. My dad may be one of Boston's most well known celebrities, but to me he's my Tuesday night date and my biggest supporter.

THE POTTER TALES

As humiliating and juvenile as it may sound, the one consistent activity that has comforted and contented me throughout my four years of high school is the reading of my bedtime story. Every night, without fail, my last wakeful moments are consumed by fantastic adventure, mystery, love, and heartbreak completely unrelated to my own life. Even as I trudge through Shakespeare, Dostoevsky, and Chaucer in my English classes, only one author sings me to somnolence. The creations of J. K. Rowling will forever haunt my dreams.

Harry Potter never fails to soothe my muggle mind every stressful day of the year. So great is my undivided devotion to this fantasy that every wall of my room displays one of the four movies modeled after my favorite stories. Yet these novels designed for the average preteen do not merely entertain me. The multicolored bindings of the books are the brooms that sweep me off to a world where magical images are more diverse than a box of Bertie Bott's Every Flavor Beans. The multifaceted nature of each Hogwarts year inspires me to search for a new phrase or interesting fact within the folds of ink-spattered parchment that make up each book. I am impressed and awed by the sheer detail Rowling commits to her fabricated world. Her Dickensian knack for intertwining minor characters and subplots is a skill I consider especially laudable. I have never thought of myself as someone who is skilled with words, which makes me appreciate Rowling's cleverness and wit even more. Take the character of Sirius Black, for example. This man, Harry's godfather, is a secret Animagus who has the ability to turn into a large black dog. Is it a coincidence that his name is shared with the constellation Sirius, which resembles just such a shaggy beast? I think not. Then there is Professor Lupin, whose lupine tendencies as a werewolf are revealed in his name. The puzzle-like pieces of the plot of Harry Potter are matched by the layers of meaning stacked like spellbooks in Rowling's language.

I go to sleep each night with my Harry Potter series on my bedside table with a deep sense of pride. While my report cards get tucked away in a drawer, and my SAT prep books collect dust under my bed, my Prisoner of Azkaban calendar remains displayed on my door. The gripping narrative of Harry Potter is my comfort food, my punching bag, and my safety blanket. I have realized that reading through fast-paced Quiddich matches and O.W.L. exams will never get old. Through tests, volleyball matches, breakups, and band concerts, I will always have an escape route through the lives of Ron Weasley and Hermione Granger. So it is with bravery, the most important attribute of a true Gryffindor, that I admit my favorite activity lies somewhere in between the worn pages of a children's story.

A STICK OF BUTTER

Lady's Chicken Noodle Soup is not just your average soup, for there's a reason behind the rhyme of its making. Paula Deen is a lovable, charismatic star on the Food Network who shares not only her recipes, but also her heartwarming stories. Paula creates her special chicken soup with a twist, seasoned with tales that reach out to viewers across the world. After suffering twenty years of devastating setbacks, including the deaths of her parents and deep financial losses, Paula spent years in shock, fear and denial. All she had were her two sons and the single activity that kept her going through the years, cooking. One day Paula "woke up," as she said, able to see things clearly. Wanting to give her life wings, Paula started a business based on her love of cooking. As "The Bag Lady," she made bagged lunches which included all of her specialties,

particularly her "Lady's Chicken Noodle Soup." Her

sons delivered the lunches to children at school and

to men and women stuck in their offices. Now the star

*of **Paula's Home Cooking**, she and her sons own a res-*

taurant called The Lady and Sons. Paula brightens

people's lives with her delicious concoctions and her

words of wisdom. She often throws a stick of butter

into almost every dish because "you can't go wrong

with butter!"

When Paula's charm and inspiration get me going, there's no turning back. I just can't help myself, for I love to cook. During the preparation of any dish, I carefully trace Paula's every move, from which knife she uses to slice the carrots to the way she so elegantly pulls the meat off the chicken. By simply watching Paula reach out to her viewers I recognize that she is teaching a valuable lesson that's more than about cooking.

Last year, I was diagnosed with epilepsy, a medical condition that could have changed my life forever. At first, I was shocked and panicked, just as Paula had been many years ago, but I remembered what she did. Paula did not let those horrible events "ride in the saddle" of her life and determine her fate. Neither will I. Okay, so I have to take pills every day. So what? Life is like one of Paula's recipes. It requires careful preparation, keeping an eye on the stove, and a dazzling presentation. And that's the way I'm going to live my life.

The ingredients of my life include field hockey, track, my friends and family, and working to support various causes. Of course, there's a little dash of school, and a pinch of part time work. Paula has it right - when life slaps you in the face, get right back up and smack it back. You only live once, so you might as well make the best of it no matter what bumps you hit along the road. And if you get stuck, just remember one thing: "you can't go wrong with butter!"

MADELINE AND ME

"In an old house in Paris that was covered with vines
Lived twelve little girls in two straight lines.
They left the house at half past nine
In two straight lines in rain or shine.
The smallest one was Madeline.
She was not afraid of mice.
She loved winter, snow, and ice.
To the tiger in the zoo
Madeline just said, "Pooh pooh!'"

My name is not Madeline and sadly, I do not live in Paris. However, this iconic fictional character and I have a lot in common. Constantly letting her curiosity get the best of her and perpetually causing a scene, Madeline exhibits a fiery independent spirit. She is street-smart and confident, yet still exhibits a childlike naiveté as she begins to navigate life's adventures.

The most obvious similarity we share, full heads of blazing red hair, has been both a burden and a blessing and has helped shape the person I am today. Redheads have strong tempers. Redheads are outspoken. Redheads are passionate. In my case at least, these stereotypes are true. While many people may see these labels as a negative, I see them rather as strong reinforcements of character. Would Madeline be so mischievous if she were a blonde or brunette? Probably. Would she be so confident? Most likely. The stereotypes resulting from one's physical appearance, however, can sometimes enhance existing character traits. The fearlessness I discovered during my many adventures riding untrained horses has translated into courage to speak my mind. The curiosity I have about the world around me has been enhanced by my willingness to ask questions and to fail. Finally, my strong sense of independence has been supported by my confidence when out in the world around me. Madeline is sincerely undaunted by the tiger, but at least in my case it would be the redhead spirit that causes her to flaunt this feeling, exclaiming, "Pooh pooh!"

Being a redhead has taught me to thrive on the strengths of being unique. Now, whenever I am separated from the norm for reasons other than my hair color, I am not uncomfortable or ashamed. Having endured such cracks as, "Julia, the red part of the rainbow came down and hit you on the head," since grade school, I feel that being a redhead has given me the confidence and inspiration to express and stay true to myself.

Madeline and I also share a connection to Paris and all it represents. After recently visiting the city that contained Madeline's "old house in Paris...covered in vines," I came to realize that this magical place is the center of a culture that has become one of my most significant passions and interests.

Ever since I was a little girl I have been fascinated by art. I have matured from an eight-year-old reading Lives of the Artists in the school library to a seventeen year old gaping breathlessly at Degas' L'etoile in the Musee D'Orsay in Paris - with many stops in the darkroom and at the easel in between. It was during this recent visit that I realized I wanted to pursue the knowledge and exploration of art for the rest of my life. I spent the majority of my time wandering through museums alone. The work of the old masters awakened me to the possibility of majoring in art history. If nothing else, my love of art has taught me that self-expression is of the utmost importance.

Perhaps here, Madeline's and my similarities end. She is, after all, a storybook character limited to a preordained life contained in a few short pages. My story, thankfully, remains to be written. With Madeline's spirit in mind, and my own self-determination, I look forward to creating my own tales, making my own mischief, and hopefully becoming one more redhead who makes her own indelible mark in the world

QUESTION:
"WHAT IS ACTING?"

ANSWER:
"EMBODYING THE INTENTIONS OF A PLAYWRIGHT."

I always play the whore. Fortunately for me, that is not all I can do. Acting has always been a main part of my life, and I strive to explore all parts of the craft as I develop as an actor. My favorite roles are those in which I am able to completely lose myself and become a character far different from who I am.

I have always thought of myself as a comedic actress, and I have not had much experience with straight roles. For example, this year I was cast as Yente the Matchmaker in *Fiddler On The Roof* . . . definitely not the whore, but an over-characterized old Jewish woman with a distinct Russian accent. You would think that it is more difficult to grasp such an outlandish character, but I find that characters such as these are easier to master than the characters that are similar to me as a person. Recently I was cast as Whitney, a tall, slender, reserved Vassar graduate in *A Piece of My Heart*. This play told the story of six women's experiences as nurses, "doughnut dollies," and as performers during the Vietnam War. The process of molding to this role was more subtly complicated than the more drastic characters that I am used to. During the process of understanding this role, both Whitney and I grew.

After performing in *A Piece of My Heart*, I have learned that there is more depth to my acting when I go beyond my comfort zone of comedy. Having to find relations between the character and myself makes me more vulnerable and forces me to really play honestly towards the intentions of the playwright. Just as vulnerability helps you let go of your own character and embody another, it also helps in analyzing a script. While studying Whitney's character, I discovered moments within the text that implied the various minor struggles that she endured. Throughout the play, for example, my character Whitney is brought down from being a Vassar graduate to a doughnut dolly. She is seen as only capable of pouring Kool-Aid and serving donuts, and because of this she searches for acceptance and attention from men. Discovering these aspects of her personal needs between the lines of the text, I had to find ways to relay these insecurities as reasons for her ultimate fall into alcoholism.

Embodying the intentions of a playwright means recognizing the writer's intentions for each of his/her characters within the text. It is the actor's job to find these intentions and to portray them honestly. Sometimes I am asked to play more provocative characters because of my look and the way that I carry myself - confidently and maturely. When I am cast for my performance and not for my physical appearance, I instinctively find ways - such as speaking with an accent and altering my physical stature - to hide myself. Yet when I am able to understand my feelings, and how they relate to my character, my performance is the most honest reflection of the text. No matter what my acting style, I know that type casting may follow me throughout my career. But perhaps it can be seen as progress that my director recently decided to cast me as whore number two instead of whore number one in *Les Miserables*.

A TRADITION OF SISTERS

"Green and White combine to stand as sisters, the bonds
of comradeship which never break, we are all connected
through family, the genes reflected in the heart of Thomp-
son Lake."

-Camp Fernwood Song

I have lots of sisters - camp sisters and real sisters.

This makes for a complicated family tree, one that is

constantly sprouting new leaves. At home my sisters

Katie and Melanie look up to me, which is both fun

and unnerving. I love that I am a role model, but at

the same time I feel the pressure of that. This year Katie

is starting high school and I will show her the ropes.

When Melanie started Fernwood Camp, I taught her

the songs beforehand. I help my sisters with adjust-

ments I have already made. I know they appreciate my

help, but might not tell me outright! They do tell me, "I

177

love you", and make me Superman dolls, cat pillows, and button bracelets.

My sister Katie is tall and trips all the time because she hasn't found her center of gravity yet. In the past year we have become best friends, singing show tunes, watching Friends, and trying to figure out our parents. Melanie is a little tomboy growing into a blonde bombshell. Melanie thinks that she owns the big chair in the living room. Everyday is a fight to see who gets to sit in it. It is amazing that we three sisters are so close. When I was little, I could always be found wearing a floral dress, tights, and a headband. On the other hand, my sisters Katie and Melanie grew up wearing ripped jeans, button down shirts, and baseball caps. While Katie and Melanie were out climbing trees and getting dirty, I spent my days playing with Barbies and doing my makeup. Although Katie, Melanie and I differed completely growing up, we have all recently connected, and our sister bond has gotten stronger.

Five summers at traditional old-fashioned 48 Camp Fernwood Lane has provided me with sisters from all over the world, ranging from quiet little Hannah who barely says a word, to drama queen Kyra, who loves to be the center of attention. Campers new and old spend the summer forming big and little sister bonds that last a lifetime. An 86-year-old camp like Fernwood fosters close relationships. Away from the stresses and distractions of day-to-day life, we are free to play, sing, get silly, and invest in lasting friendships. We are lucky to have so many great sisters and know that in our extended family, there is always room for sisters on the family tree.

M y N e i g h b o r h o o d

In an unobtrusive corner of my house sit three colorful

and worn dollhouses. These silent palaces of play are

caked in a thin film of dust and coated in a rich layer

of memories. I smile when I look upon them, for I see

my own fingerprint smudging the walls of the yellow

townhouse, my own handwritten signs decorating the

Victorian Inn, and my own clumsy little-girl sewing

providing the most luxurious tapestries for the castle.

I know and love these houses; I played with them regu-

larly until well into my freshman year of high school.

I received my first dollhouse - the classic Victorian Inn - for my tenth birthday. What wonders it provided me! The garden of stories I had mentally cultivated for years bloomed in the dollhouse. I would play for hours, not content to merely arrange my dolls around the fireplace, the table, or the bed. My dolls had personalities, had heartaches, had hubris. They had names and jobs, families and passions. My imagination would wander for hours whenever I knelt in front of the dollhouse, peering in at my beloved families inside.

My second and third dollhouses - the magic castle and the yellow townhouse - became additional "homes" when I was twelve. Most girls my age were putting their own dollhouses away, packing dolls and petite furniture in cardboard boxes that would grow old in the basement. They traded dolls for makeup, stories for gossip. I was not quite ready.

My dolls grew as I grew. The plots of my stories thickened; boy and girl dolls paired off, dances were held at the castle. My dolls would be intellectuals, I decided. They were Latin scholars, studying the subtle differences between gerund and gerundive. They were biologists, memorizing the properties of algae. I read *A Tree Grows In Brooklyn* to them and I imagined them laughing with me when Francie and Neely won the Christmas tree and crying with me when Johnny died. I spoke French to them, loving the way the words sounded as they rolled off my tongue.

Playing with my dollhouses on Saturday mornings until I was almost fifteen was a simple pleasure, but it kept me young. In this fast-moving modern world, little children grow up so fast. After a certain age, it seems that there is no longer any time or place to develop an imagination, no reason to create stories that will never be written, no excuse to crouch joyfully in front of a child's toy in a five-foot-ten-inch body. I loved playing with my dollhouses because I could make my own rules and tell my own stories. I was fully content to adopt the old-fashioned lifestyle of the inhabitants of the Victorian Inn. I was completely satisfied that the biggest scandal in the dollhouse village was that Charlie (the cook's son) and Genevieve (the princess) had held hands at the last dance.

I drew away from the dollhouse village when I was finally ready to make the transition from childhood to adolescence. My plastic "friends" made my shift so easy; all I had to do was shut the door. I won't forget the hours I spent whispering stories to the dolls and giggling to myself, or the vocabulary that I learned while teaching "school" to the dolls. I'm glad to know that these echoes of my youth remain, sitting so silently and unobtrusively, always ready for a visit.

TIPS FOR PARENTS WITH CHILDREN ATTENDING A MIDDLE SCHOOL DANCE

"OFF-EN-BACH-ER! OFF-EN-BACH-ER!" This was the deafening chant that erupted from the stands filled with frenzied soccer fans, myself included, as defenseman Matt Offenbacher made contact with the ball during the division II state championship game. Like many other spectators, I came dressed in multiple layers, ready to brace bitter autumn temperatures to witness the boys soccer team compete in their first-ever state championship in the history of Westborough High School. While my peers came armed with face paint to mark up their wind-burned cheeks with players' numbers, my supplies consisted of a pen and a pad of paper. Not only was I there to cheer; but I was there to cover

the game from the fans' point of view for the column

I'd been writing for the last five years for the Westbor-

ough News. During halftime, I went on a search for

students in the stands to interview and picked out one

of the biggest sports nuts I knew. When I called his

name and beckoned for him to come down, he gave me

a look that spoke to me as "no way are you're making

me leave my seat, with a view a spectator only dreams

about, left unattended for the taking."

"I want to interview you for my column!" I shouted. His scrunched-up, irritated face relaxed and he made his way down the bleachers. Before leaving, though, he made sure to turn around and glare at everyone who dared to steal his prized seat.

I wasn't always this determined to get a quote. When I started in 8th grade, I never mentioned to anyone that I wrote my own column. I was embarrassed at that age to admit that I'd found a passion. In junior high, my mentality was blend-in, follow-the-crowd, and never-draw-attention-to yourself. The topics I covered that first year were more personal and less centered around school-related events. Part of the reason was that this allowed me to avoid spreading the word to my peers to look for me every other week in the school section. This plan was short-lived after I wrote an article entitled, "Tips for Parents with Children Attending a Middle School Dance" - the title splashed across the school section of the

Westborough News, with my picture stamped beside it. I remember looking at that picture on a Friday afternoon in autumn and not believing it was in fact me, until I read "Gibbons Gab, by Amanda Rothman," beside the headshot. Five years later, my editor still uses the same photograph for "High Happenings, by Amanda Rothman;" that thumbnail portrait of my quirky, closed-mouth half-smile that would never open to show teeth until the end of freshman year when finally my braces were yanked off.

As I listed the top five things parents should never do to their children at a middle school dance, I seemed to forget my place in society as an adolescent eighth-grade student; instead, I believed I had enough authority to advise parents on how to avoid causing extreme horrific embarrassment to their offspring. I bestowed the five commandments of parental behavior at middle school dances - the Golden Rule being: "NEVER go into the gym and wait for your child until the dance has ended."

The night of the dance - after the decorative balloons had all been trampled underfoot and couples not quite ready to declare they were in puppy love had quickly unclasped their sweaty hands - I peered into the lobby fully expecting parents' standing in one long line, like a brick wall, to show me up and say they weren't going to take advice from a 13-year-old. A warm sensation coursed through my body and flushed my cheeks as I saw students' milling around with no parents in sight. I swallowed a ball of excitement growing in my throat and I made my way through the parent-free lobby. Just as I was about to push through the double doors, a boy stopped me to say his mom had tacked my article up on their refrigerator, and told him she'd wait for him in the car, at the end of the night. He rushed out ahead of me, and trotted over to his mother's parked Volkswagen. The parents had listened to me, and I finally understood the saying, "the power of the press." My "tips" article had sparked a following from that day forth - the majority were mothers of my peers. Before long, everyone in my grade knew I wrote a column; the idea that they all could read it destroyed my main ambition in middle school: to not get noticed. My friends and classmates were not as cruel and insensitive as I'd expected them to be.

After eighth grade, I wrote fewer "tips" articles, but I could never give it up cold-turkey. Every year, I'd write at least one: tips on the best way to ask someone to the Homecoming Dance; on what to wear the first day of school; or on what to do when you get your license. I've realized that, as long as I've written for the Westborough News, I've followed my own set of tips - a list I call, "Tips for Amanda When She's Writing a Column." At the top of the list? Have fun, and try to help make the life of parents and students just a little easier.

With Whipped Cream and a Cherry on Top

Because I've spent three summers scooping and selling ice cream, I understand with deep wisdom the mechanics of creating an ice cream sundae and the technique needed to create the perfect palatable companionship of ice cream, sauce, and toppings.

There's a fine line between a purely delicious and a mediocre sundae. I see the perplexity, sometimes terror, on the faces of customers confronted by their momentous decision-making. So, you must be very thorough when ordering. First, you must decide on the flavor of ice cream - a crucial choice indeed. The flavor of the ice cream is the basis for the entire sundae, and you must build off of your choice of ice cream when you choose toppings. Much like choosing an outfit, if you decide to wear a particular shirt, you need to coordinate the rest of your apparel to suit the style of that shirt. There are many options in choosing your flavor. For example, if you are on any form of diet, stick to the low-fat, the fat-free or the sugar-free choices. Or, if you are lactose-intolerant, the option of sorbets and sherbets is available. If you are a chocaholic (you can't believe how many there are!) and need your fix, ice creams with

187

innumerable chips, M&M's, candy bars, and fudge swirls await you in luscious decadency. No matter what consistency or flavor you crave, choose your favorite and then enhance its deliciousness with your toppings. Now you're ready for the choosing of the sauce. Selecting a sauce is easier than deciding on your base flavor since the sauces, like the jacket or the pair of pants that need to match your shirt, can easily be matched up to any flavor. An ice cream with any chocolate in it is simply NOT complete without the classic hot fudge sauces dripping and oozing down its scooped, rounded sides. Likewise, a fruity ice cream, sorbet, or sherbet simply belongs with a fruity sauce - like strawberries or pineapples. And for all of the people who dream of being a five-year-old - just one more time - there are the homey choices of marshmallow fluff and butter-scotch to return you to your youthful bliss. Then comes the neces-sary whipped cream - for a sundae is never a true sundae without the freshly-whipped, buttery favorite. You must also choose the final toppings - the tie, scarf, or high-heeled pumps that make your outfit utterly complete. The options are innumerable: From jimmies to candies to nuts, you'll always find a crunchy delight to suit your taste. Last and most important, the cherry must be sited directly on top of your powdery stack of whipped cream and toppings. The robust maraschino sits on its throne and gives your sundae its inviting finish. So go ahead, dig in - but remember to grab some napkins before you start.

M R . M C C O Y

Mr. Joseph McCoy will retire in November 2004 after teaching for 28 years at Wayland High School. I had the pleasure of taking two classes with him, Honors Modern World
History during sophomore year and Advanced Placement
United States History during junior year.

Dear Mr. McCoy,

It seems strange that, just months from now, neither of us will
walk the halls of Wayland High. I feel as if I have been here forever,
with every nook and cranny echoing of memories. I'm sure you
share this sentiment with me, as you've been here decades longer
than I.

It will certainly be different next year, when you've moved on
to the greener pastures of retirement and I will be continuing my
education at college. When I'm eating lunch next fall, I will expect
to see you strolling around the dining hall, greeting your students
and asking me how I've been doing. The impact you have had on
me in these past few years that I have known you has been immea-
surable. Somehow, you managed to teach me to read, write, and
think critically and clearly, all while getting my classmates and me
excited about history. Outside the classroom, you helped me understand how to balance my life, and what makes me happy.

When I first found out I was assigned to your class sophomore
year, I was terrified. My parents, aunts and uncles all attended Way-

land and claimed that you were an excellent teacher. I found this hard to believe, especially because I had heard from upperclassmen that you were the toughest teacher in the school. And perhaps you are; but the challenges you laid before me have only enhanced my skills.

On the first day of class most of my fears were quelled as you dubbed me "Captain." Each class after that was filled with interesting and demanding questions. You assigned us a term project for every quarter, which at first seemed insufferable. Yet, by the end of the year, you had reversed my opinion of the projects. In the fourth term I decided to write a paper about Raoul Wallenberg. Instead of sending me to the library, you gave me a novel to read about Wallenberg's life. This book, of course, read like a novel instead of a textbook and got me really interested in the subject. For the first time in perhaps my entire life, I was actually excited to be writing a paper. The only sticking point was the thesis. Instead of just telling me a thesis I could use, you asked me questions that eventually led me to a thesis. You continued this practice into my junior year. This line of questioning ultimately led me to understand how to create a thesis on my own. You, more than any other teacher, have helped me develop my critical writing and thinking skills. Ever since elementary school, I have been taught that one's writing should contain an introduction, three body paragraphs, and a conclusion. You were the first teacher to really challenge this strict structure and help me write both creatively and analytically. Despite this, you never let me forget that "A statement without evidence is worth a pitcher of warm spit."

Your assistance in the development of my critical thinking skills was only made possible by your ability to excite the class and get everyone enthusiastic about the subject. For example, to teach us about the Constitutional Convention, you sent out invitations sealed with wax, and the class acted out the Convention debates. Even at the perfunctory Saturday classes, which you held monthly to ensure that we were prepared for the AP exam, kids were always excited to attend.

Besides all of the schoolwork, you helped me just as much outside the classroom as you did within it. As time has gone by, we have spent more and more time outside the classroom, talking about school, sports and life. You're a bit like my parents in that you can sense when something is wrong and you know how to address it. I remember once before class started, you noticed that I was upset. You called me outside and postponed the start of class to ensure that I was all right. We talked about what was bothering me and somehow that brief conversation managed to clear everything up.

In my entire high school career, I have never been so close to or so impacted by any other teacher. Your enthusiasm for your job has awoken in me a love for history. But you have taught me so much more than when the French-Indian War was, or who was the twenty-second president of the United States. Through my interactions with you, I have learned to become a critical writer, reader, and thinker. I know these skills are crucial because they can be applied to so many more areas than just history. It is almost impossible for me to imagine what my experience would have been if you had not been there to teach me, guide me, and calm me. I can only hope that when I get to college, wherever that may be, that I am able to have a bond with a professor that is as strong as the one that exists between us.

Sincerely,

Laura

THE JOY WILL BE
WHAT'S IN YOUR HEART

"Okay, look in the mirror and hold your pencil verti-

cally up to your face so you can measure where your

nose begins and ends," my grandfather, with one eye

closed, explained to me. He was teaching me how to

draw facial features in perspective. We sat at the kitch-

en table - a few pieces of plain white paper scattered

over his polished sketches, nearby my rather scary dis-

oriented drawings of lips and ears.

"Michelle, to capture the human figure correctly, you need to map out the oval-like shapes and the horizontal lines: five lines for the head, one oval for the neck, a couple for the torso, and three for the arms, in order to build an organized muscle-structure." He spoke with a kind and wispy voice. My grandfather was a part-time portrait artist. He captured images with brilliantly colored messy pastels and sometimes, not often, streaky oil crayons.

When I was little, my grandfather and I sketched together whenever we visited. We'd sit down inside our home in Massachusetts or outside his home in Florida - the balmy air all around us - and he'd teach me about perspective, proportion, and texture. Some of our lessons included configuring three-dimensional boxes, faces, or trees. One time I sat next to him outside on our lawn, while he copied a tree-frog from a photograph onto his pastel canvas - drawn with caution and yet a quick steady hand, one stray mark possibly ruining the desired image. He thought carefully about what he'd next place upon the paper and blended his colors with an extended index finger. I watched him with intense interest, thinking I could never be as great an artist.

When my family visited my grandparents' apartment in Lake Worth, Florida, the space was small; and so my brother and I slept in a small room next to the kitchen. At that time, it was a bedroom with a trundle-bed and a dresser; later, turned into an office. Portraits hung on the walls of random models who'd posed over the years for my grandfather - people of different ages and ethnic backgrounds, often sitting in chairs, with varying foregrounds, backgrounds, objects, or clothing. They were amusing to stare at, just before I fell asleep. Often I made up imaginary stories about who the models were and what their lives were like, since I never knew the truth. I pictured my grandfather's sitting before his easel, with his pastels, trying to sketch this unknown model - the center of attention in a class filled with utter strangers. I thought about how long these portraits took to create and how much effort he put into them to make them look just that way.

When I was little, occasionally I sat down and drew. I loved playing with colored pencils and markers; my pictures were in good fun, nothing serious. However, when my grandfather saw them, he began to place value on them and instilled in me the belief that I had talent. He always said that I had an eye for color; he recognized I could put colors together exceptionally well, and he urged me to continue to practice and develop my skills.

From my youngest years, people around me noted my love of

art and color. Recently, my mother told me, "We used to sit down every night before bed, while I read the book Color Dance to you." She recalls that I only enjoyed the illustrations - rather than the actual story content. She reminds me that I used to change my clothes five times a day, just to express myself with different colors, textures, and patterns. My father remembers my pink plastic case, which I'd carry around wherever we went, filled with colored markers and crayons. He remembers, too, that my birthday parties most often centered around craft-related activities.

As I grew older, I began taking art classes. I took Art Workshop at school, and art course after art course. I began experimenting with different forms of art and different mediums. I'd doodle on class notes. My U.S. History teacher observed, right off, that my notes were frequently covered with strange and intricate designs and small pictures. I discovered that I liked working in pencil best - constructing pictures with 2B, 4B, and HB lines.

Anyone who visited our downstairs bathroom usually noticed, commented upon, and sometimes reluctantly complimented the "Holocaust Survivor" drawing hung on the black-and-lime green tiled wall above the toilet. Often they'd say I had a lot of talent, but, truly, I doubted my abilities. I thought my drawings were just okay, since the only people I could compare my work with were my peers in art classes. I always thought that was no real context.

Recently, my grandparents visited; and I was lucky enough to receive my annual "Lecture of the Day" from my grandfather. We met at our familiar kitchen table, at which we'd met so many times, and I showed him my newly-constructed portfolio, containing all my work, wrapped in protective clear-plastic sheeting. As we spoke about college, since I'd be heading off in a year, he asked whether I planned to major in Art. He closed by saying, "Michelle, you know that you can do whatever you want, but if you really enjoy art, do it for yourself. Don't do it for anyone else; the joy will be in what is in your heart, and your bringing it out." Whether as a major or a minor, as my vocation or avocation, I know art will always be a part of my life.

A LETTER TO MY TWIN SISTER
JULY 11, 2005

Dear Erika,

You have been gone approximately three-and-a-half days and I am already facing boredom and a nagging sense of loss. Throughout the seventeen years we have shared together, we have never been separated for more than one or two days at a time; now you will be in Guadeloupe for a month. Each day, as I head off to work in the research lab, I try to imagine what your days consist of as I prepare myself for a long day studying cells and proteins using oddly named techniques like 'Western blotting' and 'immunofluorescent staining.' My work is fascinating, yet I'm struck by how completely different my new experiences must be from your foreign adventure. It saddens me sometimes that we are unable to directly share our new encounters with each other as we always have until now. This sadness has not changed my daily routine, but I confess that sometimes when I view myself in the mirror I do not feel complete. To compensate, I conjure up memories of our escapades and adventures, and of the little moments we so frequently share. Not that the times have always been filled with perfection; there have been moments when shoving you out the closest window has seemed quite inviting. However, I catch myself in the reflection smiling and remembering that our tempers usually cool quickly and that death will not necessarily resolve a dispute concerning clothing - we can share the troublesome jeans. Through this brief separation, I have become more acutely aware that our relationship is rare and special. I can understand better why it is often strongly admired and even envied by friends and family who witness our closeness and the admiration we share for one another.

This twin bond of ours is so concrete, mutually enriching and indestructible. Our closeness helps us give each other support in school. It is always reassuring to know that I have a permanent study partner to help decipher knotty math problems, to debate the possible meanings of some moment in history, and to discuss the nuances in a novel. You reassure me on the cross-country course and the lacrosse field just by your presence, and now, even when we are thousands of miles apart and can only speak briefly on the telephone, I still easily feel this special connection. Our complex relationship cannot be explained straightforwardly, which is why I am always at a loss for words when asked how it feels to be a twin. Though we are asked this question frequently, my responses never feel precise enough. However, I know that to be a twin is a gift - a special relationship that will unite us throughout our lives and that will help us generate the strength to heal the difficulties we will face both together and separately, even when we move out of our family home to pursue more independent lives.

With your absence, Erika, I have had the chance to reflect on myself in juxtaposition to you. Just as I have become more acutely aware that our relationship is extraordinary, I have also gained a sharper sense of how we differ and of my own strengths and talents. In a way that might not be immediately obvious to most people, our connection and intimacy has provided me with a window through which to view my own unique qualities, skills, passions, and temperament. We were born on separate days, a fact we enjoy revealing, and having separate birthdays is a metaphor for the ways we have developed as unique and distinctive individuals despite being twins. There are the obvious things about me: I love to read novels, whether it's Sophie's Choice or One Flew Over the Cuckoo's Nest or One Hundred Years of Solitude; I enjoy the camaraderie and competition of lacrosse, and I crave quiet time spent drawing. Stylistic traits differ between us, too. My style is to be tenacious, somewhat quieter, but deeply committed to my pursuits; I thrive on the daily challenges that make evident the progress in both my personal and school life. We are both enthusiastic about and committed to academics, but I am especially passionate about art and activities that allow me to use my hands as well as my head. In contrast to your love of French and community service activities, I am drawn to many forms of art. Painting, drawing, photography, and ceramics all help define me as an individual - the abstract stroke of a paintbrush, the knack for precise timing that allows a special moment in space and time to be captured with the click of the camera shutter, the ability to mold a mound of clay into a recognizable object - I love these private ways of expressing myself. Art promotes feelings of calmness, sensitivity, and devotion in me.

Our separation has taught me more about myself in juxtaposition to you and in this way I have gained valuable knowledge and strength from your absence. I will be ecstatic when you return; however, the distance has given sharper definition to my own individuality and strengths. This brief separation has strengthened my sense of myself as a unique, independent, and determined person. I still hope and expect we will end up at college together, but I know we will pursue and share our own strengths and interests together wherever we land. So, dear sister, hurry home - we have lots to catch up on—and, oh, all right: you can have first choice of the jeans.

I love you!
Lizzie

What I Know Now:
A Letter to My Younger Self

Dear Sophia,

You are an amazing young woman, and I know that you are still finding yourself in the world - don't worry. You have wonderful years ahead of you; please don't grow up too quickly. You have parents who love you and want the best for you. Be kind to them. When they ask you to go with them to a new restaurant, and to visit the Museum of Fine Arts, don't resist so much. It hurts to have someone you love push you away, as you will soon learn. You are never too cool for your family, even when they call you "sweetie" in front of your friends. Your friends don't find your parents embarrassing. I know that you want to grow up quickly, but not too quickly. You have such high expectations for yourself - you imagine confidence and sophistication - and that is wonderful. The image of you now, a dark haired, pensive girl of eight, will mature into a smiling young woman wearing high heels and pearls, but the insides will develop even more.

Learn to love that your family is international - you will meet people in your school who have never tried mangoes, or eaten fresh coconuts, or even heard of jalebis or gulab jamun. I know that sometimes you feel a little left out or strange at school because of your Indian blood, but soon you will make friends with people from other countries, and people who, while they are American, deeply value their families' backgrounds and histories. Remember all of the nights when your parents tucked you into bed and read to you from the book of Indian short stories. Be proud that you have the opportunity to explore two open worlds; embrace your family on the other side of the world, and learn about their culture. Your heritage is unchangeable, and it is always with you. Let it be a gift.

You are heading into a world of change as you grow up, and I want you to know that experimenting is okay. Try new activities, new sports, new music, and new clubs. A lot of the girls around you will start to wear makeup and become image conscious - that's fine. You should feel free to try out new styles and "try on" new images. Just make sure that you feel beautiful in your own skin. Every woman has gone through the same phases you are going through, so feel free to ask for help. I know that you want to make your own way, but sometimes you need someone who knows more. Ask your mom. She will help you grow and develop, and she has the wisdom of someone who has been there and done that.

Try new activities, as they offer great ways to meet new people and discover your passions. Consider dance lessons, field hockey, and gymnastics. Try swimming - I promise you will love it! (I remember how great it felt to come in 1st place in the swimming championships after only a few months training in butterfly.) Read those Harry Potter books. Go out and talk to people - the people you approach in new situations may end up becoming your best friends. Start working early - you will love the freedom and high expectations that come with having some money of your own. Take some moderate risks. My biggest regrets are things I didn't do, and my biggest motivation is knowing that I will always wonder "what if?" What if I had never been bungee jumping? I wouldn't have realized my desire for adventure. What if I had never eaten that fried cricket on Bug Day in third grade? I wouldn't have the appreciation for such delicacies that I have now. What if I had never added a second foreign language to my schedule and found a passion for French and French culture? I certainly wouldn't have been able to get along in Paris! What if I had never read *Lord of the Flies* and *The Giver* and discovered an interest in government and society?

The years ahead are going to be full of choices. You don't need to know everything about yourself right now; you have years to figure that out. You do, however, need to know how to help yourself and get help. You need to know where your comfort zone is, and when to push outside of it. You need to know who your friends are and on whom you can rely. You need to build bridges, and the hardest choices may include knowing which bridges to build and which to burn. You need to forge relationships with the adults in your life, especially your teachers and the parents of your friends. Just be yourself, and everyone will love the beautiful young woman you are becoming.

With all of the love in the world,
SC

*Inspired by *What I Know Now: Letters to My Younger Self*, edited by Ellyn Spragins

Book Club

I met my eight closest friends, not on the playground or in the cafeteria, but instead in a world of literature. Together, we nine girls have ridden on the back of a Big Friendly Giant, walked into Little Rock High School with Melba Patillo Beals, and sat on cushions retelling one of a thousand Arabian tales. As our group has traveled through time and space from the days of Merlin to the land of The Phantom Tollbooth, we have learned the meaning of friendship, love and learning. In second grade, our mothers started a mother-daughter book club. The only thing we girls had in common was our homeroom teacher, Mrs. Brown, but we came to find connections in our appreciation of mysteries, our loathing of fantasy and our passion for reading.

Every month, we rotated houses and books. Our meetings were filled with cookies, tea, and hide-and-go-seek and always started the same way, with the question, "Who liked the book?" When we were in second grade, our analyses of the book were only as complex as "Which character did you like the best and why?" but our discussions have currently reached a level of maturity for which I am sure our mothers are relieved.

One of my fondest memories was a discussion we had while reading the autobiography of Louisa May Alcott. We were discussing friendships and my friend Maddie made a comparison between our group of girls and a rug. She explained that the Oriental rug was made up of individual pieces and colors of fiber, each playing a different role in the overall pattern. While this was an extremely precocious statement for a ten-year-old, it could not have been more accurate. This group of women has been my core unit for eleven years, guiding me through school, Sunday soccer games, museum visits and most importantly my love for reading. It has been these books of my childhood that have not only given me a world of adventure, but also a world of enthusiastic, devoted and caring friends with whom I can share this passion.

Dr. Korsunsky's
Water Pistol

On my first day of Freshman Honors Physics, my teacher set a student's desk on fire. He poured isopropyl alcohol on its surface and, to the horror of the student sitting there, ignited it, apparently demonstrating his displeasure that the student's older brother had dropped his advanced course. Dr. Korsunsky's quirky sense of humor became apparent on that first day. His favorite demonstration of the force of gravity was to simply drop a pencil from his hand onto his desk and wave his arms in glee. He forbade his students to refer to exams as tests, and instead demanded that they be called "OTA's," or Opportunities To Achieve. He awarded correct answers by hurling lollipops at unsuspecting students, and he stashed a water gun in the top

207

drawer of his desk, in order to squirt anyone foolish

enough to appear drowsy in class.

I was never a target for Dr. Korsunsky's water pistol, because I was never bored by the subject that he taught. Dr. Korsunsky's wild antics were enough to interest me in physics on the first day, but since then, I have developed a genuine love for the subject. My passion for physics helped me succeed in my freshman course and win the physics award for highest grade-point average, and has led to my desire to pursue physics in college. The study of physics provides me with a framework in understanding how the world actually works. Before Dr. Korsunsky, gravity was a mystery to me, waves existed only in the ocean, and projectiles behaved somewhat like Roadrunner cartoons: zooming straight forward off a cliff, slowing to a halt, realizing that they were in the air, and plummeting downward. I now understand that a projectile, whether it is a javelin or a spitball, follows a graceful arch. If I see a leaf falling, I know that in a vacuum, gravity would accelerate it at a rate of 9.8 meters per second squared. I adore physics because it is everywhere; as I learn more about it, the world becomes my classroom.

Whenever my family goes skiing, I drop snowballs off the chairlift, approximate the height of the chair, and calculate the speed with which they hit the ground. I recently read about a student of applied physics at Michigan who pursued a more advanced experiment, using ammonia gas to power a car on a trip to San Francisco. The University of Michigan clearly accommodates not only the brightest physics students, but also those who share my excitement and curiosity about the subject. I would be one of those students who attends voluntary "Saturday Morning Physics" lectures, or joins the Society of Physics Students. I would especially love to participate in the Society's annual "Physics Palooza," in which I could share hands-on experiments and physics toys with kids. In addition, the Undergraduate Research Opportunity Program (UROP) provides the best resources I could hope for as I advance my research from snowballs to astrophysics or elementary particle physics.

I AM NOT AN OSTRICH

I am not an ostrich. I do not like to stick my head in the sand and ignore the world around me. I am an owl. Well, not in the sense that my head can actually spin around 360°, but in that I like to take notice of all my surroundings and the happenings they contain. From wavelengths, to printed-paper, and even billions of light dots, I utilize all forms of information to obtain knowledge of the world in which I live, the world in which we all live.

Every morning, while getting ready for school, Boston's local *Matty in the Morning* radio show on Kiss 108 FM is playing on my stereo system. The naturally chatty trio composed of two middle-aged men and one young woman combine to create an interesting delivering of the day's events. I am able to hear the weather, the extent of the traffic on the Tappan Zee bridge, the score and highlights of the last night's Red Sox game, and even what new trouble the famed and fortuned have wound themselves up in.

As I stop by my kitchen table to grab a cup of coffee before running off to school, I am often surprised by newspaper and magazine clippings my parents have cut out for me, things which they think I will enjoy reading. I flip through cutouts of *The Brookline Tab* containing score reports of our boys soccer team, girls swim team, and even who has been newly elected to student council. Those are usually the least interesting because I already know most of the information through word of mouth and high school announcements. But occasionally, my parents cut out very interesting tid-bits that I otherwise would have missed. There, sitting at my place on the kitchen table, are articles on the design of the new ICA building, or columns on "what to tell your child when applying to schools this fall," even items containing recipes from the newest Gourmet magazine, instructing the reader how to make "the best Thanksgiving stuffing" or the most scrumptious chocolate soufflé. These are the things I most enjoy reading, because they are the ones which I would search for myself if I had the time.

On the weekends I have time for newspapers. I split my reading; some in *The Boston Globe* and some in *The New York Times*. *The Boston Globe* fulfills my more frivolous interests. I read up on the exact stats of the Red Sox, pretending I truly understand what all the numbers mean. I flip through the *Living Arts* section, seeing what new exhibits are up at all the local museums, and what movies have received good reviews. I then move on to more serious matter, catching up on what Governor Deval Patrick has done in the past week, or the most recent actions of senators John Kerry and Edward Kennedy. I make sure to always look at what Alex Beam had to say, and save the front page for last. I think this tradition started because my parents always read it first, and I was third in the pecking order, but now it is just tradition.

When I move on to *The New York Times*, I like to read the front page first. I then go from front to back, skimming through all the pictures, and fully reading the articles that catch my eye.

They range from new policies in Iraq to a malpractice suit against Brigham and Women's Hospital. Finally, I reach the *Week In Review* section in the Sunday edition. I read all of this. It includes which handbags are "hot for fall" but also things like details of Hillary Clinton's renewal of the infamous Health-Care plan that had previously died before it reached Congress during her husband's administration. Also interesting are the articles in this section like "The Politics Behind the Peace Prize" or "Could Afghan Poppies be Painkillers for the Poor?". If I am finished reading the paper, and my parents are still sitting out on our porch reading it as well, I often see other articles that catch my eye, that I then go back and read. I often miss information in the *Arts & Leisure* section because I read those things in *The Boston Globe*. However, I never miss *Sunday Business*, the *National Report* or the *Travel Section* (the articles on adventures by Hilary Howard are my favorite). Howard is almost as interesting as Op-Ed reporters Ellen Goodman and Maureen Dowd (also the author of one of my mother's favorite books, *Are Men Necessary?*)

At night, I switch to television. I mockingly mimic the CW's *News at Ten* spiel of "it is ten o'clock, do you know where your children are?" And make it a point to yell up the stairs to either one of my parental units: "It's ten o'clock, do you know where I am? I am in the den watching TV!" They pretend to be amused. I then proceed to channel surf through various stations. Watching parts of *The Hills* on MTV and then moving onto channel 55, shows like *The Daily Ten* and *The Soup*, are, I am embarrassed to say, slightly amusing as they either mock the stars or sympathize with them. Don't worry, I usually have better taste in television. When not watching the news or cruddy reality shows (which I really do not watch that often), I skip to dramas like *Grey's Anatomy* and *House*, or even *Prison Break* or the classic, *Law& Order*.

Once I have had my fair share of news, or mindless television, I can proceed to bed - to be woken in the morning by the heinous jangle of my alarm clock, but then calmed by *Matty in the Morning*, the smell of coffee, and more magazine clip-outs.

Hope Perches in the Soul

I have to been to Lebanon ten times in my life. I have visited for just a few weeks at Christmas and have pictures of me with my family standing next to mounds of snow and beneath a 2,000-year-old cedar tree. I have gone at Easter and stayed up all night with friends and family until we all finally went to church together at five in the morning. Since I was 12, I have spent every summer roaming the narrow and winding streets of my father's village and eating fresh burgundy figs in the early morning.

On July 24, 1990, my parents married in a small ceremony in a church in northern Lebanon. My mother, a Shiite Muslim, and my father, a Catholic, exchanged vows in front of my father's parents and siblings in the final year of the civil war. No one in my mother's family was in attendance. It was a small and simple wedding. My parents married against both their families' wishes because they understood what no one else did: It is about more than religion and politics.

I witnessed the summer war between Israel and Hezbollah in 2006. I heard and saw air strikes and lived in fear for a week and a half. For fifteen years, my parents lived through a civil war that pitted Muslims against Christians filled with gunfire, car bombs, and weekly massacres. They have seen it all. They saw Lebanon at its best in the 1960s, a top tourist destination with a flourishing economy, and they have seen it at its worst, a war torn nation divided along religious lines. Since 1975, Lebanon has had rare moments of peace.

Emily Dickinson once wrote, "Hope is the thing with feathers that perches in the soul." To me, though, my parents represent everything Lebanon should be and everything that I hope to make it one day. They married in the hope that one day, Christians and Muslims could truly coexist, marry, raise children, and together build a better future. They married in the hope that churches and mosques could occupy the same quarter of downtown Beirut. They married in the hope that people will no longer pick up arms over religion. They may not agree on everything. In fact, they don't agree on much to this day when it comes to politics, but at the core of their beliefs is one dream.

I am sure that every night when they close their eyes they dream the same dream. They see red tile rooftops and ancient stone seaports. They see a mountain range with flowing waterfalls and snow-capped mountaintops. They see stretches of taupe sand and azure water, and they see the most brilliant sunsets over the Mediterranean Sea. One day that is what Lebanon will be known for, and I hope to have played an active role in that dream.

The Importance of Tangential Questions

When I was a fifth grader, my teacher never called on me. She had become fed up with my permanently raised hand and my constant questions - which didn't always apply to what we were talking about at that moment. Eventually, she handed me a brand new yellow pad and a bright blue pen. "Mel," she said, "Whenever you have a question, I want you to write it down here." By the end of each class I would have pages and pages of questions.

"Why do we use X and Y as variables?"

"When a plant isn't in the sun, how long until it dies?"

"How, exactly, do blue and yellow combine to make green?"

My teacher told me to just keep the questions in my desk. She probably intended to return to them one day, but she never answered them. My questions about early algebra and photosynthesis and pigmentation festered in my desk drawer and creating them grew into a habit. When any sort of question came up in my mind, I couldn't stop myself from wondering more and more about the subject.

My curiosity followed me into the art world. I remember a trip to MOMA in New York City when I was in seventh grade. One of the first paintings I saw was a large black and white canvas with the words "CATS IN BAG BAGS IN RIVER." The questions were rapid firing in my head! Was this art? What was the artist trying to evoke? I probably could have done a similar painting if I had a stencil and a blank canvas! The Christopher Wool painting left me perplexed. Was that the purpose of this avant-garde art, to simply confuse the audience? As soon as I got home I went on the Internet and searched everywhere for the meaning of this painting. Finally, I found it: the printed line was from the 1957 movie Sweet Smell of Success. "CATS IN BAG BAGS IN RIVER" was a code phrase used by one of the characters to indicate that an evil deed had been done. I learned that the artist was inspired by the poetry and the sinister terseness of the phrase in creating this work of art. My MOMA experience opened up an entirely new way of looking at art. My appreciation of contemporary art began to form and enhance my understanding of more traditional paintings and drawings. While my first thought of this painting was "What's so special about this? I could have done it," the painting has left a lifelong impression on me about the power of images to convey messages. This year, I experimented with my own art containing political messages around the historic presidential election. I created a satirical piece intended to provoke thought about Sarah Palin as a vice presidential candidate. I share the political philosophy of Shepard Fairey, the artist who created Obama's HOPE poster, which is "question everything." I now see art as a powerful medium for asking questions.

My questions can reveal fascinating details about people. This year for my history class, we went to a retirement home to interview senior citizens who had lived in Massachusetts in the 1920's and 30's. I was assigned to Rose, a ninety-seven year-old woman who could not remember much. But what she could remember, I found compelling. We had a page of questions that my teacher had handed to us; we were instructed to follow it exactly. While the questions our teacher assigned were basic and interesting, I couldn't help but trail off and ask my own questions. "What were your friends like?" "Did you ever get in any kind of trouble?" Over two hours went by and I hadn't finished asking all of the assigned questions. Yet I felt like I had learned a great deal about Rose and the time period that she lived in. I learned about how her dad punished her with a belt strap when she was caught smoking in the barn with her friends. I learned that there were even harsher punishments for failing to perform simple chores such as milking the cow. While I did get the responses to the assigned questions about her parents and the level of her education, her responses to my inquiries about her teachers and boyfriends were much more revealing. I began to realize that my unassigned questions went to the heart of what it meant to grow up as a young woman in Boston just before the Great Depression.

My questions probe the edges of the universe! Every Fourth of July, we go out on a boat with our family and friends to watch the fireworks just outside of New Bedford. This past year, the sky was clearer than ever before. My inquisitive nature got the best of me again as I pondered about the stars and the universe, and what is beyond all of that. I started to wonder about the tiny place we hold in the universe. I wondered if maybe, just maybe, our entire civilization could be as small as a grain of sand in another, bigger world where there is life. Looking into that night sky, questions flew into my mind that no one could answer for me. "How did people measure just how far away the planets are?" "Might extraterrestrial beings see us, floating offshore, beneath the exploding bottle rockets and roman candles?" I have a bank of unanswered questions, including some of those written on yellow paper and shoved in my desk drawer a long time ago. I've realized that while they can be frustrating, unanswered questions create space for my imagination to conjure up some of the many possibilities - for delight, for truth, for beauty - that exist in this world.

THE FIRST DAY OF SCHOOL

The dirty aged train pulled to a stop where my grandmother - age 6 - stood. It was the fall of 1941; it was my grandmother's first day of school - the day she'd long looked forward to. But the train was not there to take her to school. It was there to strip the little girl of her freedom and hoist her away from the village she knew and loved. An order had gone out to deport the Jewish people from her village in Poland to the Ukraine. The jammed train rocked forward and began its grim trip west across the flat land of Poland and into the strange towns of the Ukraine. She never made it to school that day.

Flash forward fifty years. By contrast, my first day of school can be viewed on a fifty-one inch television screen in our home in Carlisle, Massachusetts; you can see the moment of departure either in VCR or DVD versions. The camera, held by my mother, bounces just a little as she proudly waves goodbye to me, but otherwise the experience of a happy little girl headed off to her first day of school can be seen clearly. Boldly, I mount the three enormous steps of the handsome yellow school bus that will escort me to my first day of growing up. I will learn to read from beautiful short books that overflow the school library, filled with colorful pages and magnetized illustrations. I will learn to write lowercase, uppercase, and cursive script on sheets of large-ruled lined paper.

For my grandmother - her freedom nonexistent - her childhood nonetheless continued to thrive as she was taken across the Ukraine, held at one camp after another. With her yearning to be in school still burning and unsatisfied, she asked people around her to teach her to read and write. They did so, using their fingers as their only writing utensils and the dirt of the earth as a chalkboard.

Although our upbringings were vastly different - as is the way we learned to read and write - my grandmother and I are more similar than any other two people I know. We are joined by our strong love of literature and writing. Our love for literature and writing guides us through worlds of wisdom and knowledge. At the entrance to the Museum of the Diaspora in Tel Aviv, a small sign reads: "A people set out on a great journey with only a Book as its guide." I think of two little girls, separated by fifty years, joined by a Book, all books, joined by the written word, and a love of language.

Last summer, I spent a month in Ukraine with my family retracing the tedious trail my grandmother was forced to follow. It was really then that I realized how abundant an American life I have led, a life so different from my grandmother, my ancestors, and even relatives living abroad today.

My grandmother had to march for endless miles through the Ukraine, a country foreign to her, because Evil never saw her as a little girl who wanted just to go off to school and learn to read and write - just as I, the other little girl, had wanted to, in Carlisle, Massachusetts, fifty years later.

Our town-by-town trip through the Ukraine followed my grandmother's every step. It concluded at that point when, finally, after several years, she was rescued, and shipped at the war's end to Rumania and from there to a life in Israel, with a family and always with her books.

My New England town, so close to Concord, Massachusetts, makes a great deal out of Patriot's Day (April 19), which marks when the American Revolution began, and the Fourth of July, Independence Day. People are decked out in Colonial era costumes; there are parades and re-enactments. Since returning from the Ukraine to my beautiful New England town, still looking so much as it once did at the time of the American Revolution, with farmlands and rolling hills, I view those holidays a little differently. I know more clearly the rights, protection, and safety that came from what happened on the days those holidays celebrate. Probably always for me the lesson will reduce itself to two little girls ready for the first day of school, and how in America you take for granted a proud parent's wave, a school all ready to welcome a eager young learner, and a safe yellow school bus to take you to school - and bring you back home again, where you belong.

WHAT CAN A THOUGHTFUL MAN HOPE FOR MANKIND ON EARTH, GIVEN THE EXPERIENCE OF THE PAST MILLION YEARS?

One answer, according to Kurt Vonnegut's prophet in **Cat's Cradle**, *Bokonon, "consists of one word and a period . . . Nothing." There are days when I think this less-than-cheery outlook fits the less-than-cheery nature of the world that I, and my generation, find ourselves in: a war overseas that has lasted nearly half my lifetime; domestic and international poverty that, through images, has an impact like a punch to the stomach but then is almost immediately forgotten or ignored; and rampant persecution of "Those Who Are Different".*

"Forget peace," people say, because conflict can't be solved through diplomacy, compromise, or discussion. The death of innocent bystanders is an acceptable price for the continuation of a war. The psychological effects on the children and refugees and communities inflicted by a raging war are negligible and easy to overcome. Adults and newspapers tell me that idealism is only for the young, and that as one gets older it degenerates into sturdy realism. Or at least, that's what happened to many of those adults. And if it happened in the past, it'll happen in the future, no matter how much I try to guard such foolhardy idealism. I can't even vote, so should I even speak up? I'm a teenager, not the president of the United States. Despite being lucky enough to live in a democracy, the common American youth often feels he or she has no power to effect change.

"Forget humanitarianism," people say, because bumbling American do-gooders do more harm than good. Since concrete results – the end of erosion! Increased electricity from disorganized governments! A halt to teenage pregnancy! – are far more important and measurable than abstract ones – "cultural understanding?" "personal growth?" "youth leadership?" – such supposedly empowering efforts are meaningless. The summer after my sophomore year, I traveled to the Dominican Republic for two months. At first, I was very concentrated on quantitative achievement, measured in the number of lessons taught or the amount of money raised. However, by the end of my two months in a community, I placed a much higher value on my new relationships and cross-cultural cooperation. After returning from the Dominican Republic in 2007 and Panama in 2008, I have struggled to avoid the conclusion that because humanitarianism does not eliminate poverty, ineffectual governments, or environmental degeneration in one fell swoop, I would do better to sit at home and laze on my couch and ignore my own ignorance of other people and places.

"Forget acceptance," they say, because tolerating people who don't look, act, think, or live like you is a pipe dream. Barriers – of barbed wire, or of lines on a map, or of prejudice – are built to Keep Them Out. Shouldn't we be bothered when children passively take on the prejudices of their parents? In my childhood, I mentally cruised along until a book was assigned in seventh grade: Elizabeth Laird's Kiss the Dust. Early in the book, a Kurdish boy is shot on the street by an Iraqi police officer. I was shocked and I didn't understand it, but Middle Eastern issues are so complicated that trying to understand is often billed as a pointless pursuit. As a human being conscious of other human beings' suffering, I am torn between the lure of inaction and the responsibility to bring awareness to their cause, or to speak up against something I think is wrong.

But – wait! It occurs to me that Bokononism is a self-professed pack of lies. Lies that make us happy and content, but lies nonetheless. If we hope for nothing, we don't need to work for any goals. We're never disappointed. We accept the repetition of war, poverty, and injustice, simply because it once was and so shall be again, and there's nothing we can do to change that.

With all due respect to those who have already given up, I like the truth better. Truth: I can't solve war, poverty, and injustice – or at least, not by myself. Truth: What can I, along with my generation, achieve? What can I, a thoughtful person, hope for mankind on earth? One word and a period:

Everything.

CPSIA information can be obtained at www.ICGtesting.com
Printed in the USA
BVOW08s0123280515

402209BV00004B/17/P